SOUPS
FOR ALL
SEASONS

Brad McCrorie

1987
DOUBLEDAY CANADA LIMITED, TORONTO, ONTARIO
DOUBLEDAY AND COMPANY INC., GARDEN CITY,
NEW YORK

Copyright © 1987 by Brad McCrorie
First edition

Recipe testing by Claire Stancer
Cover photography by Jeremy Jones
Design and Illustration by N. R. Jackson
Typesetting by Trigraph Inc.
Printed and bound in Canada by Freisen Printers

Canadian Cataloguing in Publication Data
McCrorie, Brad
Soups for all seasons
ISBN 0-385-25136-X
1. Soups.   I. Title.
TX757.M22   1987   641.8'13   C87-094082-1

**Library of Congress
Cataloging-in-Publication Data**
McCrorie, Brad.
Soups for all seasons
1. Soups.   I. Title
TX757.M42   1987   641.8'13   87-13385
ISBN 0-385-25136-X

INTRODUCTION

For Brad McCrorie, there is no meal or occasion, indeed no celebration imaginable that cannot be greatly enhanced with homemade soup. And whether your appetite tends toward the hot and hearty soups of winter, or the cool and refreshing soups traditionally associated with summer dining; whether it's a robust meal-in-a-bowl, a chunky chowder, or a creamy oyster stew that is called for, or delicate, savory clear broths or bouillon, you need look no further than the pages of this book for a recipe.

Here are fifty delicious, nutritious, economical, and easy-to-prepare recipes from the 28-year-old caterer and culinary whiz whose "soups-of-the-day" have become a tradition at his parents' deli. A visit to the deli is a highlight of market day for a growing number of fans among the close to 20,000 people who weekly visit the historic St. Lawrence Market near Toronto's harborfront. It is here, five days a week, throughout the seasons of the year, that the word of mouth continues to grow (appropriate advertising for homemade soups!) as the loyal and the curious stop by Gert's Deli to read the hand-lettered chalkboard announcing Brad's tempting, inventive, and always satisfying creations.

The secret to making really great soups, according to this energetic young chef, is homemade stock. "With homemade stock and market-fresh ingredients," he says, "you simply can't go wrong." (McCrorie's recipes

1

for flavorful and wholesome soup stocks can be found on pages 10, 11, and 12.)

Market-fresh ingredients, for Brad McCrorie, means food in season, a subject which, if given half a chance, he will talk about for hours on end. Like farmers' markets everywhere, Toronto's St. Lawrence Market celebrates the seasons of the year with a colorful and constantly changing variety of fresh meat, poultry, and produce from the surrounding farmlands of Ontario and from around the world. Whenever asparagus or fiddleheads first pop their green goodness through the black earth of spring—whenever the first avocados, melons, blueberries, or plums are in season and ready for picking anywhere, their arrival at the market is heralded, according to McCrorie, with a sense of joy that ordinary supermarket shoppers will probably never understand.

There is a basic difference between people who market and people who merely shop, true foodies say. It has something to do with the fresh, unwrapped displays, the tables piled high with beets, leeks, and radishes, their greens still attached, the mounds of lettuce and cauliflower, the bulging baskets of newly ripened corn. But it is also the sense of being a part of, and taking part in, the whole food experience: chatting with old friends and meeting new ones, getting to know the merchants, the farmers, the bakers, butchers, and fishmongers by name. It's getting to know the difference between hothouse tomatoes and those that have ripened on the vine, and learning when cantaloupe or honeydew melons are at their best. It's picking out the freshest fish, and tasting a sausage you may never have heard about before. It's all of this, and more than this, they'll tell you here.

"Sure you'll find new potatoes, baby carrots, fresh broccoli, and watercress in supermarkets," say those people for whom marketing is a weekly event, a fun-filled family outing akin to visiting an actual farm. "Of course, when spring lamb goes on sale, or the first Atlantic salmon arrive, you'll find them everywhere. But it's not the same."

Brad McCrorie understands the difference between people who market and people who shop. "Show me people who like to market, and I'll show you people who like to cook," he says. "These people know food. They want to see it out from under its plastic wrap where they can touch it, test its weight in their hands, almost taste it."

These people, he says, don't want butchers or fishmongers telling them what size of cuts of meat or fish are available, or how many sausages come in a pack. They have a particular meal in mind. They come to the market to select fresh spinach, green beans, or snow peas for a romantic dinner for two or a feast for four special friends—not portions prepackaged for other appetites.

People who shop to create a special meal, people who will spend time at a market stall selecting the fresh herbs and spices they want to make a meal come alive, will enjoy this book. For in the words of a long-time fan of the fun and foodstuff that a market represents, these people shop for their weekly groceries in much the same way that Brad shops for the ingredients for his distinctive soups, goulashes, gumbos, chowders, and stews. Of course, like Brad, they start with a recipe or a menu in mind, but, also like Brad, they shop wisely, seeking out not just fresh produce, but the freshest, best-tasting food of all.

As the talented creator of two (often three or four) soups daily, more than 250 days a year, Brad's repertoire of recipes is varied and vast. The selection of fifty for this book was not an easy task, but it was an enjoyable and rewarding one involving many tastings and retastings.

Here they are: clear soups, cold soups, fish chowders, creamed soups, thick and fancy soups— arranged by season, and all using the peak seasons for fruit, vegetables, meat, fish, and poultry throughout the twelve months of the year.

As they say at Gert's—enjoy!

SOME TERMS
AND TECHNIQUES

All the recipes in this book are quite simple to make. However, there are some special ingredients, terms, and procedures with which you may be unfamiliar. Here, then, is everything you need to know to make wonderful soups.

BEURRE-MANIÉ

Serious cooks are never without a pound of this excellent soup or stock thickener in the refrigerator. Beurre-manié, kept in this fashion, should always be brought to room temperature before using. Simple to make, beurre-manié is equal parts of whole butter and hard white flour, kneaded by hand until the resulting mixture is of a smooth consistency. Since the flour is raw and likely to lump if added to hot liquid, the soup or stock is added to the beurre-manié a little at a time, while stirring constantly until the mixture is consistent and ready for adding to the pot. It is wise to remember that raw flour does have a starchy taste, and that all recipes calling for beurre-manié require thorough cooking to remove this taste.

UNSALTED BUTTER

Since the addition of salt to any food or soup is ultimately a matter of taste or diet, the recipes in this book were tested using unsalted butter. Salted butter, for those who prefer it, can be substituted.

CLARIFIED BUTTER

This is butter from which the butter fat and milk solids have been removed. It is made by melting butter over a medium-high heat, then skimming off or straining the solids from the resulting liquid. Used for flavor and color when browning or frying, clarified butter gives the cook the ability to cook longer, at higher temperatures, without burning.

COMMERCIAL BASES

Since time is an important ingredient in any cook's plans for dinner, and since few people have enough of it to devote to the proper reduction of the stocks used in the soup recipes in this book, there is no harm in adding one or two tablespoons of commercial base for added flavor when and where time and taste dictate.

ADDING CHEESE OR EGGS TO SOUP

Cheese is only added to cream soups or soups that contain plenty of garnish for the cheese to cling to. Cheese is always grated before it is added to the boiling broth. Eggs must be added slowly with a whisk while the soup or stock is boiling. Soups may also be thickened without flour by a *liaison* of equal parts egg yolk and whipping cream (35 percent). This mixture should be added once the soup has been brought to a boil and whisked slowly (not whipped) with the heat reduced to a simmer.

ADDING CREAM TO SOUP

To avoid curdling or separation, stock or soup should be properly thickened before you add any cream. The recipes in this book call for 35 percent cream because it gives a richer taste and more full-bodied texture to soups, and is less likely to curdle than other creams.

DRIED MUSHROOMS

Some of the recipes featured in this book call for dried mushrooms. This has been done simply because dried mushrooms are available all year round. There is really no substitute for fresh mushrooms when and where they are available. Dried mushrooms should always be soaked for at least an hour at room temperature in water that has been brought to a rapid boil, then removed from the heat. Since the stems of dried mushrooms are apt to be tough, always trim the ends of the stems, or remove the stems altogether.

FREEZING SOUPS

Since cream added to the stock in the preparation of creamed soups is apt to separate in freezing, it is best not to freeze creamed soups. However, you can always freeze the stock from which you plan to make a creamed soup. When the soup is thawed, add the cream to the stock when it comes to a boil. Since crisp vegetables will not be crisp when frozen and later reheated, and since eggs will discolor, clear soups should only be frozen after straining out these ingredients. Fresh vegetables or eggs can then be added, according to the recipe, once the stock has been thawed and brought to the proper temperature.

REDUCTION

Stocks, soups, and even wines are reduced by simmering to increase, strengthen, or concentrate their flavor. Reductions called for in each recipe (one-half reduction/one-quarter reduction) are achieved by simmering the liquid over a medium-high heat to the desired strength.

ROUX

Light or dark, roux are easy to make and are often used to thicken soup. Both call for equal parts of butter and flour blended gently over a slow heat until the flour is cooked completely enough to rid it of its starchy taste. For the rich, nutty flavor of dark roux—used in thick, dark, and gamey soups—cook the roux over a medium-high heat until it turns a rich brown color.

SAUTÉ, SWEAT

As the difference between a light roux and a dark roux is the amount of cooking involved, so is it the difference between sweating and sautéing foods to be added to soups. To sauté is to cook food rapidly in hot butter or fat, turning and tossing it until it is golden brown, thereby sealing in the juices. To sweat is to bleed the juices from vegetables by stirring them gently in hot butter.

SERVING SIZES

All the soups in this book will yield 8- to 10-ounce servings—perfect for lunch, pre-dinner, or a meal at any time.

STOCK AND DEMIGLACE

Following are three basic recipes used throughout the book: chicken stock, beef stock, and beef demiglace. Recipes that use special vegetable, fish, poultry, or game stocks have the stock recipe included with the soup recipe.

BASIC BEEF STOCK

3 lbs	beef bones	1.4 kg
2	onions with skin, quartered	2
2	carrots, cut in 2-inch (5-cm) pieces	2
3	garlic cloves	3
2	stalks celery, cut in 2-inch (5-cm) pieces	2
2 tbsp	tomato paste	30 mL
12 cups	cold water	3 L

Preheat oven to 450°F (250°C).

    Place bones in a shallow roasting pan. Roast in preheated oven until they begin to brown, about 30 minutes. Add onion, carrots, garlic, celery, and tomato paste and continue to roast about 30 minutes more or until bones and vegetables are dark brown.

    Combine browned bones and vegetables with water in a large stock pot. Bring to a boil over medium-high heat. Reduce heat to medium-low and simmer for 1 to 2 hours, skimming off the foam as it appears, and adding more water as necessary to keep the level constant. Strain out bones and vegetables.

YIELDS 12 CUPS (3 L).

BASIC CHICKEN STOCK

4.4 lbs	chicken bones	2 kg
2	onions with skin, quartered	2
3	carrots, cut in 2-inch (5-cm) pieces	3
3	garlic cloves with their skin	3
2	stalks celery, cut in 2-inch (5-cm) chunks	2
2	bay leaves	2
¼ tsp	dried basil	1 mL
¼ tsp	dried oregano	1 mL
¼ tsp	dried thyme	1 mL
1½ tsp	white peppercorns	7 mL
5	sprigs of parsley with their stems	5
16 cups	cold water	4 L

Put chicken bones, onion, carrots, garlic, celery, bay leaves, basil, oregano, thyme, peppercorns, and parsley into a large, heavy stock pot and cover with water. Bring to a boil over high heat, then immediately reduce heat to medium-low and simmer for 1 or 2 hours (or longer), skimming off the foam as it appears and adding water as necessary to keep the level constant. Strain out bones and vegetables and discard them.

Return stock to pot, raise heat to medium, and cook until stock has reduced by about a quarter, about 30 minutes.

YIELDS 12 CUPS (3 L).

BEEF DEMIGLACE

$^1/_3$ cup	unsalted butter	75 mL
$^1/_3$ cup	hard or all-purpose flour	75 mL
8 cups	beef stock	2 L

In a large, heavy soup pot, melt butter over medium-high heat. Then whisk in flour and continue to cook, whisking constantly, until flour is golden brown, about 5 minutes. While whisking, pour in $^1/_2$ cup (125 mL) of stock at a time until mixture is smooth, and simmer until thickened slightly, about 5 minutes more.

YIELDS 8 CUPS

SPRING

SPRING

The first day of spring is one thing, and the first spring day is another. The difference between them is sometimes as great as a month.

Henry Van Dyke

Suddenly or slowly, however it happens where you live, winter ends, and as the days grow longer in the march toward the summer solstice, the season of plowing and planting is once again magically followed by the arrival of fresh local produce in the market. The world is green, the seemingly endless haul from the festive season of Christmas and New Year's through the February blahs is over. There are new sights, sounds, and smells in the air. Farmers' markets everywhere are alive with the excitement. There is a spring in everyone's step, people are smiling, and the taste buds are eager to try something new.

CREAM OF
CHICKEN
WITH DIJON MUSTARD
AND CAPERS

*This wonderful soup will become an instant favorite
with family and friends. It is a delightful choice for
spring evenings.*

¹/₄ cup	unsalted butter	50 mL
2 3-oz	chicken breasts, finely diced	2 85-g
1 cup	finely diced Spanish onion	250 mL
¹/₄ cup	finely diced sweet red pepper or pimento	50 mL
¹/₄ tsp	minced garlic	1 mL
¹/₄ cup	dry sherry	50 mL
2 tbsp	dry white wine	30 mL
1 tbsp	finely chopped capers	15 mL
2 tbsp	Dijon mustard	30 mL
¹/₄ tsp	dried tarragon	1 mL
6 cups	chicken stock	1.5 L
5 tbsp	beurre-manié	75 mL
¹/₂ cup	whipping cream (35 percent)	125 mL
¹/₄ tsp	dry mustard	1 mL
	salt to taste	
	white pepper to taste	

In a medium-sized, heavy soup pot, melt butter over medium-high heat until it turns a nutty brown color. Add chicken and sauté 3 or 4 minutes until it turns opaque. Remove to a plate with a slotted spoon and set aside. Add onion and red peppers and sauté 3 or 4 minutes or until onion begins to color slightly. Add garlic and continue to cook 30 seconds more, stirring constantly. Stir in sherry, wine, capers, Dijon mustard, and tarragon; bring to a boil. Add the stock, return to boil, then reduce heat to medium, and cook for 10 minutes.

In a medium-sized bowl, whisk beurre-manié until smooth. Slowly whisk in 1 to 2 cups (250 to 500 mL) of soup mixture until beurre-manié resembles a smooth paste. Whisk into the soup mixture 1 spoonful at a time. Simmer gently to thicken slightly.

Stir in chicken and cream, and season with dry mustard, salt, and pepper. Bring to a boil and serve immediately.

SERVES 6 TO 8.

LOBSTER BISQUE
WITH ARMAGNAC

Available live, cooked in the shell, fresh cooked or frozen, lobster is always guaranteed to please guests. This rich, smooth bisque with aromatic armagnac is always a hit.

STOCK

1 lb	live or frozen lobster	450 g
¼ cup	unsalted butter	50 mL
1	celery stalk, coarsely chopped	1
1	small onion, coarsely chopped	1
2	cloves garlic, chopped	2
1 tbsp	ground Spanish paprika	15 mL
1	bay leaf	1
1½ tsp	dried tarragon	7 mL
⅓ cup	armagnac	75 mL
¼ cup	dry sherry	50 mL
7 cups	chicken stock	1.75 L

SOUP

¼ cup	unsalted butter	50 mL
1 cup	finely chopped onions	250 mL
1 cup	sliced mushrooms	250 mL
2 tbsp	finely diced sweet red pepper or pimento	30 mL

¼ tsp	dried tarragon	1 mL
3 tbsp	hard white or all-purpose flour	45 mL
1 tbsp	armagnac	15 mL
1 tbsp	dry sherry	15 mL
¼ cup	whipping cream (35 percent)	50 mL
	salt to taste	
	white pepper to taste	

If using a live lobster, place it on a flat pan to reserve juice from cutting. With a sharp knife, sever the vein at the base of the neck. Divide the body at the tail and cut tail into 3 or 4 pieces. Divide the shell into 4 pieces.

To make lobster stock, heat butter in a heavy medium-sized stock pot over high heat. Add lobster and sauté until it turns bright red, stirring frequently. Reduce heat to medium-high, add celery, onion, garlic, paprika, bay leaf, and tarragon; sweat until onion becomes transparent, about 2 to 3 minutes. Add armagnac and ignite immediately with a match to flambé. Once the flame is completely out, stir in sherry and chicken stock. Bring to a boil, reduce heat, and simmer for 10 minutes. Remove lobster to a plate to cool, then pick the meat from the shells, dice, and set aside for soup. Strain stock and set aside. There should be 6 cups of stock.

Heat butter in a heavy, medium-sized soup pot over medium-high heat. Add onions, mushrooms, red pepper, and tarragon; sweat until onion becomes translucent. Whisk in flour to make a white roux and cook about 1 minute. Slowly whisk in lobster stock ½ cup (125 mL) at a time until smooth, and simmer until thickened slightly. Stir in armagnac, sherry, cream, and lobster meat, and season with salt and pepper. Serve immediately.

SERVES 4 TO 6.

SHARK BISQUE
WITH BOLETS AND SHERRY

An unorthodox and unusual bisque to say the least, is this zesty creation, combining shark meat with garden herbs and sherry. The dill gives the bisque a spring-like flavor.

¹/₄ cup	dried bolet mushrooms	50 mL
1 cup	boiling water	250 mL
¹/₄ cup	unsalted butter	50 mL
1 lb	shark meat, diced into 1-inch (2-cm) cubes	450 g
2 cups	diced Spanish onions	500 mL
¹/₂ tsp	minced garlic	2 mL
¹/₄ tsp	finely chopped fresh dill	1 mL
¹/₂ tsp	dried tarragon	2 mL
¹/₃ cup	dry sherry	75 mL
6 cups	chicken stock	1.5 L
6 tbsp	beurre-manié	90 mL
¹/₂ cup	whipping cream (35 percent)	125 mL
	dash Worcestershire sauce	
¹/₄ tsp	ground nutmeg	1 mL
	salt to taste	
	white pepper to taste	

Cover mushrooms with water and soak until soft, about 1 hour. Drain, slice, and reserve liquid.

In a large, heavy soup pot, heat butter over medium-high heat until it is a nutty light brown color. Add shark meat and sauté 3 to 4 minutes or until opaque. Remove with a slotted spoon and set aside. Add mushrooms, onions, garlic, dill, and tarragon; sweat for 3 to 4 minutes or until onion is translucent. Stir in sherry, bring to a boil, and reduce by half. Add stock, bring to a boil, reduce heat to medium-low, and simmer for 10 minutes.

In a medium-sized bowl, whisk beurre-manié until smooth. Slowly whisk in 1 to 2 cups (250 to 500 mL) of the soup mixture until beurre-manié resembles a smooth paste. Add to the soup 1 spoonful at a time, whisking constantly. Simmer until thickened slightly.

Stir in cream and shark meat and season with Worcestershire sauce, nutmeg, salt and pepper. Simmer 5 minutes or until shark is completely cooked.

SERVES 8 TO 10.

CREAM OF
RED SNAPPER

If fish soup is what you crave, red snapper is one of the most superbly flavored fish available and always in good supply at fishmongers throughout the year. Brad's cream of red snapper has long been a favorite with his fans and will win fans for you. It makes a good prelude to a light spring supper.

STOCK

3 lb	fileted red snapper (reserve bones for stock) cut into ½-inch (1-cm) chunks	1.4 kg
10 cups	cold water	2.5 L
1	small onion, chopped	1
1	stalk of celery, diced	1
½ tsp	dried thyme	2 mL
2	bay leaves	2

SOUP

¼ cup	unsalted butter	50 mL
1 cup	finely diced onions	250 mL
1 cup	finely diced leek	250 mL
¼ cup	finely diced sweet red pepper or pimento	50 mL
1 tsp	garlic	5 mL
¼ tsp	dried thyme	1 mL
½ tsp	dried tarragon	2 mL
⅓ cup	dry white wine	75 mL

2 tbsp	dry sherry	30 mL
8 cups	fish stock	2 L
8 tbsp	beurre-manié	125 mL
½ cup	whipping cream (35 percent)	125 mL
3 tbsp	grated parmesan cheese	45 mL
	ground nutmeg to taste	
	salt to taste	
	white pepper to taste	

To make the fish stock, combine fish bones, water, onion, celery, thyme, and bay leaves in a large stock pot. Bring to a boil over medium-high heat, then reduce heat to medium-low. Remove white foam as it appears, and simmer for 30 minutes only; fish stock will become bitter if left to simmer longer. Strain and set aside. Yield should be 8 cups stock.

In a large, heavy soup pot, melt butter over medium-high heat until it is a nutty light brown color. Add onions, leek, red pepper, and garlic and sauté for 3 to 4 minutes, stirring occasionally until vegetables wilt slightly. Stir in thyme, tarragon, wine, and sherry. Bring to a boil and reduce to half the amount. Stir in the stock and return to boil.

In a medium-sized bowl, whisk the beurre-manié until smooth. Slowly whisk in 1 to 2 cups (250 to 500 mL) of the soup mixture until the beurre-manié resembles a smooth paste. Whisk into the soup 1 spoonful at a time. Simmer for 2 to 3 minutes, or until thickened slightly.

Add red snapper meat and let cook in the soup for 4 to 5 minutes or until it flakes easily. Stir in cream and cheese. Season with nutmeg, salt, and pepper.

SERVES 8 TO 10.

MULLIGATAWNY

This marvelously rich soup is Anglo-Indian in origin.
The curry and chutney give it a distinctive flavor.

¹/₄ cup	unsalted butter	50 mL
1 lb	naturally double smoked pork, diced to ¹/₄-inch (0.5-cm) cubes	450 g
2 cups	diced Spanish onion (about 1 large)	500 mL
2 cups	diced leeks (about 2 medium)	500 mL
1 cup	diced carrots (about 2 medium)	250 mL
¹/₂ cup	chopped celery (about 1 small stalk)	125 mL
3 cups	peeled and diced spy apples (3 large)	750 mL
1¹/₂ tsp	minced garlic (about 2 medium)	7 mL
¹/₄ cup	medium-strength curry powder	50 mL
¹/₄ cup	parboiled, converted long grain rice	50 mL
1 tsp	dry mustard	5 mL
1 tsp	ground nutmeg	5 mL
7 cups	chicken stock	1.75 L
4 tbsp	beurre-manié	60 mL

1 cup	whipping cream (35 percent)	250 mL
¼ cup	mango chutney	50 mL
1 tsp	Worcestershire sauce	5 mL
	salt to taste	
	white pepper to taste	

In a very large, heavy soup pot, melt butter over medium-high heat. Add pork, onion, leeks, carrots, and celery and cook until vegetables are tender-crisp and slightly wilted, about 7 minutes. Add apples and continue to cook for 2 minutes. Add garlic, curry powder, rice, mustard, and nutmeg, and continue to cook for about 3 minutes, stirring constantly. Stir in stock and bring to a boil, then reduce heat to medium and simmer for 10 minutes, being sure that rice is completely cooked.

In a medium-sized bowl, whisk beurre-manié until smooth. Slowly whisk in 1 cup (250 mL) of the soup mixture until beurre-manié resembles a smooth paste. Add to the soup 1 spoonful at a time, whisking constantly. Simmer until thickened slightly.

Stir in cream and chutney and season with Worcestershire sauce, salt, and pepper.

SERVES 12 TO 14.

FRENCH VEGETABLE
AND CHESHIRE CHEESE

An excellent meal straight from the garden to your table. Fresh vegetables, with the rich, tart taste of this splendid English cheese, which was the basis for the original Welsh rarebit.

1/4 cup	unsalted butter	50 mL
3 cups	diced Spanish onion	750 mL
2 cups	diced carrots	500 mL
1 cup	sliced leek	250 mL
2 cups	chopped celery	500 mL
3 cups	coarsely chopped zucchini	750 mL
2 cups	sliced mushrooms	500 mL
1 bunch	broccoli, coarsely chopped	1 bunch
1	medium green pepper, sliced	1
2 cups	diced tomatoes (about 2 medium)	500 mL
1/2 tsp	finely diced garlic	2 mL
2 tbsp	dried oregano	30 mL
1/2 tsp	dried basil	2 mL
1 tbsp	Worcestershire sauce	15 mL
1 tbsp	granulated sugar	15 mL
8 cups	chicken stock	2 L
3 oz	linguini noodles, broken in threes	85 g

½ lb	English Cheshire cheese, grated	225 g
	salt to taste	
	white pepper to taste	

In a large, heavy soup pot, melt butter over medium-high heat. When butter begins to foam slightly, add onion, carrot, leek, and celery. Sauté for 3 to 4 minutes or until vegetables are slightly wilted. Add zucchini, mushrooms, broccoli, green pepper, tomatoes, and garlic, and sauté for 3 to 4 minutes more, then add oregano, basil, Worcestershire sauce, and sugar. Stir in chicken stock, bring to a boil, add noodles, and cook for 7 minutes. Add a handful of cheese at a time while stirring constantly until melted. Season with salt and pepper. Serve immediately.

SERVES 10 TO 12.

CREAM OF
ONION AND GARLIC

Onion, garlic, and, for good measure, leek, combine to produce this uniquely flavored salute to spring.

$^{1}/_{4}$ cup	unsalted butter	50 mL
1 cup	finely diced leeks	250 mL
5 cups	finely diced Spanish onions (about $2^{1}/_{2}$ large onions)	1.25 L
3 tbsp	minced garlic (about 9 cloves)	45 mL
2 tbsp	diced pimento or sweet red pepper	30 mL
$^{1}/_{2}$ cup	dry white wine	125 mL
8 cups	chicken stock	2 L
1 tsp	Worcestershire sauce	5 mL
1 tsp	granulated white sugar	5 mL
5 tbsp	beurre-manié	75 mL
1 cup	whipping cream (35 percent)	250 mL
$^{1}/_{2}$ cup	chicken base	125 mL
1 tsp	dry mustard	5 mL
$^{1}/_{2}$ tsp	ground nutmeg	2 mL
	salt to taste	
	white pepper to taste	

In a large, heavy soup pot, melt butter over high heat or until butter begins to turn a nutty brown color. Add leek and onions; cook over high heat, stirring constantly for 3 or 4 minutes or until onion has softened. Add garlic and pimento, continue to cook 2 minutes, stirring constantly. Reduce heat to medium-high, add wine, chicken stock, Worcestershire sauce and sugar. Bring to a boil, reduce heat to medium, and simmer for 5 to 10 minutes.

In a medium-sized bowl, whisk beurre-manié until smooth. Slowly whisk in 1 cup (250 mL) of the soup mixture until beurre-manié resembles a smooth paste. Whisk into the soup 1 spoonful at a time, stirring constantly. Simmer gently to thicken slightly.

Stir in cream and season with base, mustard, nutmeg, salt, and pepper. Bring just to a boil and ladle into soup bowls.

SERVES 10 TO 12.

CREAM OF
ONION AND STILTON CHEESE

A creamy soup with a blend of onion, garlic, and that most prized of English cheeses, Stilton. Unlike many blue cheeses, the flavor of this cheese is anything but harsh.

¼ cup	unsalted butter	50 mL
4 cups	diced onions (about 2 onions)	1 L
¼ cup	celery	50 mL
¼ cup	green pepper	50 mL
½ tsp	minced garlic	2 mL
½ cup	white wine	125 mL
1 tsp	Dijon mustard	5 mL
6 cups	chicken stock	1.5 L
6 tbsp	beurre-manié	90 mL
¾ lb	Stilton cheese, grated or crumbled	340 g
1 cup	whipping cream (35 percent)	250 mL
	dash Worcestershire sauce	
¼ tsp	ground nutmeg	1 mL
	salt to taste	
	white pepper to taste	

In a medium-sized, heavy soup pot, melt butter over medium-high heat until it is a nutty brown color. Add onions, celery, green pepper, and garlic, and sauté for 3 or 4 minutes, stirring occasionally until vegetables are limp. Add wine, bring to a boil, and reduce by half. Stir in mustard and chicken stock, bring to a boil, reduce heat to medium, and simmer for 4 or 5 minutes.

In a medium-sized bowl, whisk beurre-manié until smooth. Slowly whisk in 1 to 2 cups (250 to 500 mL) of the soup mixture until beurre-manié resembles a smooth paste. Whisk into the soup mixture 1 spoonful at a time. Simmer gently to thicken slightly.

Add a small handful of cheese at a time, whisking constantly until melted. Stir in cream and season with Worcestershire sauce, nutmeg, salt, and pepper and serve.

SERVES 6 TO 8.

GREEN ONION
AND LIME

*Although essentially a salad vegetable, the distinctive
flavor of green onion or scallions is wonderfully
enhanced with lime for this spring taste treat.*

1/4 cup	unsalted butter	50 mL
1 cup	finely diced leek (about 1 large)	250 mL
1/2 cup	finely diced celery (2 medium stalks)	125 mL
5 cups	sliced green onions (about 30)	1.25 L
1 tsp	granulated sugar	5 mL
1/2 tsp	dried tarragon	2 mL
7 cups	chicken stock	1.75 L
4 tbsp	beurre-manié	60 mL
1/2 cup	whipping cream (35 percent)	125 mL
1/3 cup	lime juice (juice of 3 limes)	75 mL
1 tsp	dry mustard	5 mL
1/2 tsp	ground nutmeg	2 mL
	salt to taste	
	white pepper to taste	

In a large, heavy soup pot, melt butter over medium-high heat or until butter begins to foam slightly. Add leek and celery; sweat until tender, about 3 or 4 minutes. Add green onions, sugar, and tarragon, and sauté 5 minutes or until green onions wilt. Stir in stock and bring to a boil, reduce heat, and simmer 5 to 10 minutes.

In a medium-sized bowl, whisk beurre-manié until smooth. Slowly whisk in 1 cup (250 mL) of the soup mixture until beurre-manié resembles a smooth paste. Add to the soup 1 spoonful at a time, whisking constantly. Simmer until thickened slightly.

Stir in cream and lime juice and season with mustard, nutmeg, salt, and pepper. Simmer for 5 minutes. Spoon into serving bowls.

SERVES 8 TO 10.

CHILLED PEANUT BUTTER
WITH FRANGELICA

*For intimate dining, and when you are out to impress,
this delicately different chilled soup is simple to make
and simply divine to eat.*

1¹/₂ cups	chunky peanut butter	375 mL
1 cup	sour cream	250 mL
4 cups	half and half cream	1 L
	(10 percent)	
3 tbsp	lemon juice (juice of 1 lemon)	45 mL
2 tbsp	lime juice (juice of 1 lime)	30 mL
¹/₄ cup	Frangelica liqueur	50 mL
2 tsp	grated lemon rind	10 mL
1¹/₂ tsp	grated lime rind	7 mL
1 tsp	granulated sugar	5 mL
	ground nutmeg to taste	
	salt to taste	

Place peanut butter in a large bowl. Whisk in sour
cream, half and half cream, lemon juice, lime juice,
Frangelica, lemon rind, and lime rind. Season with
sugar, nutmeg, and salt. Chill for 12 hours before serving.

SERVES 4 TO 6.

SUMMER

SUMMER

Summer's lease hath all too short a date.

Shakespeare

In the season of garden parties, lunch on the terrace, and backyard barbeques, soup makes perfect sense. It's summertime, and the livin' *should* be easy! Not only is soup delicious, nutritious, and easy to prepare, it can also be prepared well in advance—taking advantage of the coolest part of the day in the kitchen—and then chilled for serving later, or reheated minutes before a special meal.

At no time of year are fresh garden vegetables more abundant and less expensive than they are right now, and whether shopping city markets or roadside stands in cottage country, the wise shopper will take full advantage of this fact. And at no time of year does it make more sense to have frozen stock on hand.

When soup and sandwiches on the patio are exactly what weather and the family call for, or when entertaining your favorite friends, the following recipes for flavorful, chilled soups as well as marvelously hot and fancy dinner soups are guaranteed to please.

VEAL
WITH GRAPES AND SHERRY

This makes an interesting and unusual complement to a summer meal.

¹/₄ cup	unsalted butter	50 mL
4 3-oz	provimi veal cutlets, julienned	4 85-g
1¹/₂ cups	diced Spanish onions	375 mL
¹/₂ tsp	minced garlic	2 mL
1 cup	diced mushrooms	250 mL
¹/₄ cup	finely diced sweet red pepper or pimento	50 mL
¹/₂ tsp	dried tarragon	2 mL
1 tsp	Dijon mustard	5 mL
¹/₄ cup	dry white wine	50 mL
¹/₃ cup	dry sherry	75 mL
6 cups	chicken stock	1.5 L
6 tbsp	beurre-manié	90 mL
¹/₂ cup	whipping cream (35 percent)	125 mL
¹/₂ cup	green seedless grapes, peeled	125 mL
¹/₄ tsp	ground nutmeg	1 mL
	salt to taste	
	white pepper to taste	

In a medium-sized, heavy soup pot, melt butter over medium-high heat. Add veal cutlets and sauté for 3 or 4 minutes or until they turn opaque. Remove with a slotted spoon and set aside. Add onions, garlic, mushrooms, red pepper, and tarragon, and continue to sauté another 3 or 4 minutes, stirring frequently or until onions are translucent. Stir in mustard, wine, and sherry, bring to a boil, and reduce by half. Stir in stock, bring to a boil, and cool for 3 or 4 minutes.

In a medium-sized bowl, whisk beurre-manié until smooth. Slowly whisk in 1 to 2 cups (250 to 500 mL) of soup mixture until beurre-manié resembles a smooth paste. Whisk into the soup mixture 1 spoonful at a time. Simmer gently to thicken slightly.

Stir in cream, veal, and grapes, and season with nutmeg, salt, and pepper. Reduce heat to medium. Simmer 1 or 2 minutes and ladle into bowls.

SERVES 6 TO 8.

DUCK MONTMORENCY
WITH PORT

If the duck didn't say it, the port should. This is a dinner soup that is rich, flavorful, and filling. The perfect starter for a meal to remember.

STOCK

3.3 lb	duck	1.5 kg
12 cups	cold water	3 L
2	medium carrots, chopped	2
1	leek, chopped	1
1	medium onion with skin, quartered	1
½ tsp	dried thyme	2 mL
2	juniper berries	2
2	bay leaves	2

SOUP

¾ cup	unsalted butter	175 mL
2 cups	sliced mushrooms	500 mL
1 cup	diced green pepper	250 mL
½ cup	finely diced leek	125 mL
1 cup	diced onion	250 mL
1 tsp	minced garlic	5 mL
¼ tsp	dried rosemary	1 mL

2	juniper berries	2
1/4 tsp	dried thyme	1 mL
1/2 cup	hard flour	125 mL
10 cups	duck stock	2.5 L
2 tbsp	brandy	30 mL
1/2 cup	port	125 mL
1/4 cup	black currant jelly	50 mL
2 cups	cherries, pitted and sliced	500 mL
	ground nutmeg to taste	
	salt to taste	
	white pepper to taste	

Preheat oven to 450°F (250°C).

To make duck stock, debone duck, dice meat, and set aside for the soup. Discard skin. Break up bones and place them in a shallow roasting pan. Roast in preheated oven until dark brown, about 1 hour, turning once or twice. Combine browned bones, water, carrots, leek, onion, thyme, juniper berries, and bay leaves in a large stock pot. Bring to a boil over medium-high heat. Reduce heat to medium-low and simmer 1 or 2 hours, skimming off the foam as it appears, and adding more water to keep the level constant. This process should yield 10 to 12 cups of duck stock.

In a large, heavy soup pot, melt 1/4 cup (50 mL) of the butter over medium-high heat until frothy. Add duck meat and sauté for 4 minutes, stirring occasionally until browned. Then add the mushrooms, green pepper, leek, onion, garlic, rosemary, juniper berries, and thyme. Sauté about 5 minutes, or until vegetables begin to brown. Remove the vegetables to a bowl with a slotted spoon and set aside.

Melt the remaining butter over medium-high heat. Once it is melted, whisk in flour and continue to cook until golden brown, whisking constantly, about 5 minutes. While whisking, pour in ½ cup (125 mL) of stock at a time until the mixture is smooth and thick. Return the duck and vegetables to the pot, reduce heat to medium, and simmer for 10 minutes.

Stir in brandy, port, black currant jelly, and cherries, and continue to simmer for 5 minutes. Season with nutmeg, salt, and pepper and serve.

SERVES 10 TO 12.

MANDARIN ORANGE

WITH LIME AND FRESH DILL

A quick and easy-to-prepare cold soup for the summer;
an excellent perky treat, as refreshing as sherbet.

4 cups	fresh mandarin orange or orange juice	1 L
¼ cup	dry sherry	50 mL
2 cups	plain yogurt or sour cream	500 mL
2 cups	table cream (10 percent) or half and half (18 percent)	500 mL
½ cup	lime juice (4 limes)	125 mL
1 tbsp	grated lime rind (2 limes)	15 mL
1 tbsp	chopped fresh dill	15 mL
	ground nutmeg to taste	

Pour mandarin orange or orange juice into a large mixing bowl. Whisk in sherry, 1½ cups (375 mL) yogurt or sour cream, cream, lime juice, and lime rind. Season with dill and nutmeg. Chill for 4 hours.

To serve, ladle into soup bowls and garnish with a dollop of the remaining yogurt or sour cream.

SERVES 8 TO 10.

MUSSEL STEW
CAFÉ DE PARIS

*Fortified with brandy and red wine, tender sweet
mussels have seldom been treated more royally than in
this delicious, brothy stew. In a word, excellent!*

¹/₄ cup	unsalted butter	50 mL
2 cups	diced onion (about 1 large)	500 mL
2 cups	diced leeks (about 2 medium)	500 mL
1 tbsp	minced garlic (about 3 medium)	15 mL
2 cups	diced green pepper (about two)	500 mL
1 tbsp	tarragon	15 mL
¹/₄ cup	brandy	50 mL
1 cup	red wine	250 mL
8 cups	chicken stock	2 L
2 tbsp	chopped capers	30 mL
1 tbsp	diced anchovies (about 3 or 4)	15 mL
60	small mussels, cleaned and bearded	60
1 tsp	Worcestershire sauce	5 mL
1 tbsp	Pernod	15 mL
2 tbsp	lemon juice (from ¹/₂ lemon)	30 mL
	salt to taste	
	white pepper to taste	

In a large, heavy soup pot, melt butter over medium-high heat. Add onion, leeks, and garlic and cook until leeks are wilted, about 3 to 5 minutes, stirring occasionally. Add green pepper and tarragon, sauté for 1 or 2 minutes or until pepper has softened slightly. Stir in brandy and red wine. Bring to a boil and reduce liquid by half. Stir in chicken stock, capers, and anchovies, and bring back to boil. Add mussels. Cover and cook about 5 minutes, stirring once, or until mussels have opened. Season with Worcestershire sauce, Pernod, lemon juice, salt, and pepper.

SERVES 10 TO 12

NOTE ABOUT MUSSELS

1. To test mussels for freshness before cooking, the shell should be closed. If it is open, try tapping it against another shell. If the shell closes, the mussel is fresh, if not, discard it.
2. To clean mussels, wash them in a colander under cold running water. Scrub them with a stiff brush and pull off the beard or clip it with scissors.
3. After cooking, the mussels should open. Discard those which don't open. Be sure not to overcook mussels—this makes them tough.

MUSSEL TOMATO
CONCASSE

Three cheers for the seaside! Fresh, tender mussels
bobbing in a concasse of garden-fresh tomatoes,
exquisitely spiced for summertime.

¹/₄ cup	unsalted butter	50 mL
1 cup	diced Spanish onions	250 mL
1 cup	diced leeks	250 mL
¹/₂ cup	finely diced green pepper	125 mL
1 tbsp	minced garlic	15 mL
¹/₂ tsp	dried tarragon	2 mL
¹/₂ tsp	dried oregano	2 mL
1 tsp	granulated sugar	5 mL
¹/₄ cup	dry white Bordeaux	50 mL
5-6	tomatoes, peeled, seeded and diced (about 5 cups)	5-6
1 cup	chicken stock	250 mL
2 lbs	mussels, cleaned, beards removed	900 g
	salt to taste	
	white pepper to taste	

In a large, heavy soup pot, melt butter over medium-high heat until bubbly. Add onions, leeks, green pepper, and garlic and sauté for 3 or 4 minutes or until vegetables have wilted slightly. Stir in tarragon, oregano, sugar, and wine, and bring to a boil. Add tomatoes and stock, return to boil, reduce heat to medium-low, and simmer for 20 minutes.

Bring soup back to a boil over medium-high heat. Add mussels and cook covered about 5 minutes or until mussels have opened. Season with salt and pepper and ladle into bowls.

SERVES 4 TO 6.

SCAMPI STEPHANIE

It's hard to believe that there was a time in history when scampi were tossed back into the sea by fishermen who weren't quite sure what these shelled fish were. Today they are considered a delicacy, and few treatments bring out their light, briny, sweet taste as well as this incredible soup.

¹/₄ cup	unsalted butter	50 mL
¹/₂ cup	finely diced leek	125 mL
¹/₂ cup	finely diced onion	125 mL
¹/₂ tsp	minced garlic (1 small clove)	2 mL
1 tsp	finely chopped dill	5 mL
6	large scampi, with the skin on	6
1 tbsp	armagnac	15 mL
1 tbsp	dry sherry	15 mL
1 tsp	Pernod (optional)	5 mL
4 cups	chicken stock	1 L
1 cup	sliced strawberries	250 mL
	salt to taste	
	white pepper to taste	

In a medium-sized soup pot, heat butter over medium-high heat until bubbly. Add leek and onion; sweat for 3 to 4 minutes, stirring occasionally until vegetables are slightly wilted. Add garlic, dill, and scampi, and continue to cook for 2 or 3 minutes. Stir in armagnac, sherry, and Pernod, and bring to a boil. Stir in stock and return to a boil. Add strawberries, season with salt and pepper, and serve immediately.

Note: If scampi cook too long, they have a tendency to toughen.

SERVES 2 TO 3.

LOBSTER
WITH JULIENNE OF LOX AND SAFFRON

Lobster in the style of Provence. A perfect first course for any meal that celebrates a special occasion.

1 1/2 lb	lobster or frozen lobster	675 g
2 tbsp	olive oil	30 mL
2 tbsp	vegetable oil	30 mL
4 cups	diced leek	1 L
2 cups	diced Spanish onion	500 mL
1/4 cup	finely diced green pepper	50 mL
2 cups	sliced mushrooms	500 mL
1/4 cup	finely diced sweet red pepper or pimento	50 mL
1 tbsp	minced garlic	15 mL
1 tsp	dried tarragon	5 mL
4	saffron threads	4
1 tsp	capers, chopped	5 mL
1/4 cup	brandy	50 mL
1/4 cup	dry white wine	50 mL
2 tbsp	dry sherry	15 mL
8 cups	chicken stock	2 L
	salt to taste	
	white pepper to taste	
3 oz	lox, julienned	100 g

If using live lobster, place lobster on a flat pan so as to reserve any juice that results from cutting. With a sharp knife, sever the vein at the base of the neck. Divide the body at the tail and cut the tail into 3 or 4 pieces. Divide the shell into 4 pieces.

Heat olive and vegetable oils in a heavy, medium-sized soup pot over high heat. When a wisp of white smoke appears, add lobster and sauté until it is bright red, stirring frequently. Reduce heat to medium-high, add leek, onion, green pepper, mushrooms, and red pepper. Sweat, stirring occasionally until onion is transparent, about 3 or 4 minutes. Add garlic, tarragon, saffron, and capers, and continue to cook for 1 minute. Stir in brandy, ignite with a match to flambé. Once flames die out completely, stir in the wine and sherry, bring to a boil, and stir in stock. Bring to a boil again, then reduce heat to medium-low and simmer for 5 to 10 minutes. Remove lobster to a plate and allow to cool. Once cooled, pick the meat from the bones, chop coarsely, and return to soup.

Season with salt and pepper. To serve, ladle into soup bowls and garnish with lox.

SERVES 8 TO 10.

SHRIMP AND GARLIC
WITH MUSHROOM CAPS AND PERNOD

When the mood is right, and romance is in the air, this is the one! Succulent, tender shrimp and mushroom caps served piping hot—another perfect meal-in-a-bowl for special occasions.

STOCK

1½ lb	jumbo shrimp, peeled, cleaned, and cut into 3 (keep shells for stock)	675 g
6 cups	chicken stock	1.5 L
1	small onion, cut into 4	1
3	small bay leaves	3

SOUP

¼ cup	unsalted butter	50 mL
20	medium-sized mushroom caps	20
1 cup	finely diced onion	250 mL
1 tbsp	minced garlic	15 mL
2 tbsp	diced pimento or sweet red bell pepper	30 mL
1 tsp	dried tarragon	5 mL

1 tsp	curry powder	5 mL
½ cup	dry white wine	125 mL
2 tbsp	Pernod	30 mL
	salt to taste	
	white pepper to taste	

To make shrimp stock, combine shrimp shells, chicken stock, onion, and bay leaves in a medium-sized stock pot. Bring to a boil over medium-high heat, then reduce heat to medium-low and simmer for 30 minutes only (fish stock will become bitter if left to simmer longer). Strain and set aside. There should be about 5 cups of stock.

In a medium-sized, heavy soup pot, melt butter over medium-high heat. Add mushrooms and sauté until tender, about 4 minutes. Add onion, shrimp, garlic, pimento, tarragon, and curry powder. Sauté until onions are soft, about 5 to 7 minutes. Stir in wine, bring to a boil, and reduce to about half, about 10 minutes. Stir in shrimp stock and Pernod and season with salt and pepper. Bring to a boil and serve piping hot.

SERVES 4 TO 6.

CREOLED CLAMS

A hearty hats-off to Louisiana and the ever-increasing popularity of Creole cookery. Rich and nutritious, with garden-ripe tomatoes, it adds a Cajun touch to summertime menus.

¹⁄₄ cup	unsalted butter	50 mL
1 cup	diced green pepper (about 1 medium)	250 mL
1 cup	diced celery	250 mL
2 cups	diced Spanish onion (about 1 large)	500 mL
¹⁄₂ cup	diced leek (about 1 small)	125 mL
1 tsp	minced garlic	5 mL
1 tbsp	chopped capers	15 mL
1 tbsp	dried oregano	15 mL
1 tsp	dried basil	5 mL
¹⁄₂ tsp	dried tarragon	2 mL
¹⁄₄ cup	dry sherry	50 mL
8 cups	peeled, seeded, and diced tomatoes (about 8 large)	2 L
3 tbsp	lemon juice (about 1 lemon)	45 mL
1 lb	clams	450 g
	salt to taste	
	white pepper to taste	

In a large soup pot, melt butter over medium-high heat until bubbly. Add green pepper, celery, onion, and leek, and sauté 3 or 4 minutes, stirring occasionally, or until vegetables have wilted slightly. Add garlic and continue cooking for 30 seconds. Stir in capers, oregano, basil, tarragon, and sherry, and bring to a boil. Add tomatoes and lemon juice and return to a boil. Reduce heat to medium-low and simmer for 25 minutes.

After 25 minutes, increase heat to medium-high and return soup to boil. Add clams and cook covered about 5 minutes or until clams have opened. Season with salt and pepper and serve.

SERVES 6 TO 8.

CREAM OF
FRESH BASIL

*Fresh basil, for some people, is worth a trip across town.
We think you'll agree, once you have tasted this
excellent, creamy treat from the herb garden.*

¹/₄ cup	unsalted butter	50 mL
1¹/₂ cups	finely diced onion	375 mL
1 cup	finely diced leek	250 mL
³/₄ cup	chopped fresh basil	175 mL
¹/₃ cup	dry white wine	75 mL
3 cups	chicken stock	750 mL
3 tbsp	beurre-manié	45 mL
¹/₄ cup	whipping cream (35 percent)	50 mL
¹/₂ tsp	dry mustard	2 mL
	ground nutmeg to taste	
	salt to taste	
	white pepper to taste	

In a medium-sized, heavy soup pot, heat butter over medium-high heat. Add onion, leek, and basil; sweat until onion and leek are limp. Stir in wine, bring to a boil, and reduce to half the amount. Stir in stock. Bring soup to a boil, reduce heat to medium, and simmer for 5 minutes.

In a medium-sized bowl, whisk beurre-manié until smooth. Slowly whisk in 1 cup (250 mL) of the soup mixture until beurre-manié resembles a smooth paste. Add to the soup 1 spoonful at a time, whisking constantly. Simmer until thickened slightly.

Stir in cream and season with mustard, nutmeg, salt, and pepper, and serve.

SERVES 2 TO 4.

COOKED, CHILLED
GAZPACHO

Gazpacho, someone once said, is the soup maker's ultimate salute to summer. This one is all of that! Spicy, refreshing, satisfying, there is nothing quite like this nourishing, chilled soup on a summer day. Many people keep it on hand in the refrigerator all summer long.

¼ cup	unsalted butter	50 mL
2 cups	diced Spanish onion	500 mL
1 cup	diced carrots	250 mL
2 cups	diced celery	500 mL
2 cups	diced green pepper	500 mL
2 cups	sliced mushrooms	500 mL
2 tbsp	minced garlic	30 mL
½ tsp	dried basil	2 mL
1 tbsp	dried oregano	15 mL
30	Italian-type plum tomatoes, peeled, seeded, and diced	30
3 tbsp	granulated sugar	45 mL
⅓ cup	red wine vinegar	75 mL
½ tsp	hot pepper sauce (optional)	2 mL
2 tbsp	Worcestershire sauce	30 mL
	salt to taste	
	white pepper to taste	

In a large soup pot, melt butter over medium-high heat. Add onion, carrots, celery, green pepper, and mushrooms; sweat 3 to 4 minutes, stirring occasionally or until the vegetables have wilted slightly. Add garlic, basil, and oregano, and continue to cook another 30 seconds. Add tomatoes, sugar, and vinegar, bring to a boil, reduce heat to low, and simmer for 40 minutes. Chill for 12 hours and season with pepper sauce, Worcestershire sauce, salt, and pepper.

SERVES 8 TO 10.

CREAM OF
BRAISED LETTUCE

A creamy, hot confection that can be made with fresh lettuce in any season, but is especially delightful in summer.

¹/₄ cup	unsalted butter	50 mL
3 cups	finely diced Spanish onions (about 1¹/₂ large onions)	750 mL
2 cups	finely diced leeks (about 2 large leeks)	500 mL
1 cup	finely diced celery	250 mL
¹/₂ tsp	minced garlic	2 mL
¹/₂ cup	finely diced pimento or sweet red bell pepper	125 mL
¹/₄ cup	dry white wine	50 mL
1 tsp	Worcestershire sauce	5 mL
7 cups	chicken stock	1.75 L
1	large leaf lettuce, coarsely chopped	1
5 tbsp	beurre-manié	75 mL
1 cup	whipping cream (35 percent)	250 mL
¹/₂ tsp	ground nutmeg	2 mL
	salt to taste	
	white pepper to taste	

In a large, heavy soup pot, melt butter over medium-high heat until it is a nutty, light brown color. Add onions, leeks, and celery; sweat, stirring occasionally until vegetables are limp, about 5 minutes. Add garlic and pimento. Continue to cook for 2 more minutes. Stir in wine and Worcestershire sauce, bring to a boil, and simmer for 2 minutes. Stir in chicken stock. Bring back to boil, add lettuce, and simmer 1 minute.

In a medium-sized bowl, whisk beurre-manié until smooth. Slowly whisk in 1 cup (250 mL) of the soup mixture until beurre-manié resembles a smooth paste. Whisk in the soup mixture 1 spoonful at a time. Simmer gently to thicken slightly.

Stir in cream and season with nutmeg, salt, and pepper and serve.

SERVES 10 TO 12.

PINEAPPLE AND KIWI
WITH SHERRY

Fruit soups have been gaining in popularity in recent years and not just with the diet set. Excellent summer fare for all appetites, these light and lively concoctions always impress and keep well in the refrigerator for snacking or dining any time.

1	pineapple, peeled and cored	1
6	kiwis, peeled	6
2¼ cups	table cream (18 percent)	550 mL
¼ cup	dry sherry	50 mL
1½ tsp	brandy	7 mL
1 tsp	diced fresh dill	5 mL
	ground nutmeg to taste	
	salt to taste	

On the large blade of a grater, grate ¾ of the pineapple and 5 of the kiwis into a medium-sized bowl. Quarter the remaining pineapple and slice the remaining kiwi and set aside for garnish. Stir in cream, sherry, and brandy, and season with dill, nutmeg, and salt. Chill at least 4 hours.

To serve, ladle into chilled soup bowls, and garnish with pineapple and kiwi slices.

SERVES 4 TO 6.

AUTUMN

AUTUMN

Season of mists and mellow fruitfulness,
Close bosom-friend of the maturing sun;
Conspiring with him how to load and bless
With fruit the vines that round the thatch-eaves run.

John Keats

The Thanksgiving season. As the days grow shorter, and the cooler air of autumn calls for hearty and sustaining meals for the back-to-school crowd, kitchens come alive. Fresh fruits and vegetables are, of course, still abundant. Fresh game and spicy sausages are traditionally associated with this time of year, and glistening oysters, while available the year round, are plumper and look better than they do at perhaps any other time.

CANTONESE

BRAISED BEEF AND OYSTER

Oysters are best during the months that have an "R" in them: September, October, November, and so on. These are the months when the sea is coldest. This is an unusual soup with a Cantonese flavor.

¼ cup	peanut or vegetable oil	50 mL
1 lb	flank steak	450 g
2 cups	diced Spanish onions	500 mL
½ cup	diced carrots	125 mL
1 cup	diced green peppers	250 mL
½ cup	sliced mushrooms	125 mL
1 tbsp	minced garlic	15 mL
½ tsp	Chinese five-spice powder	2 mL
1 tbsp	granulated sugar	15 mL
6 cups	beef stock	1.5 L
¼ cup	cornstarch	50 mL
¼ cup	cold water	50 mL
¼ cup	oyster sauce	50 mL
12	fresh oysters, shucked, reserve juice	12
	salt to taste	
	white pepper to taste	

In a large, heavy soup pot, heat oil over high heat until a wisp of smoke appears. Add meat and sauté for 2 to 3 minutes, stirring constantly. Add onions, carrots, green peppers, and mushrooms, and continue to sauté for 3 or 4 minutes or until vegetables are tender-crisp. Stir in garlic, five-spice powder, and sugar. Stir just to combine, then stir in stock. Bring to a boil, reduce heat to medium-low, and simmer for 10 minutes.

In a small bowl, stir cornstarch with water until combined. Whisk into soup and continue to simmer for 2 or 3 minutes, or until soup has thickened slightly.

Whisk in oyster sauce, then add oysters and their juice. Season with salt and pepper and ladle into bowls.

Note: Be sure not to overcook oysters. They take just a few minutes to cook.

SERVES 8 TO 10.

BEEF
WITH GREEN PEPPERS

Flank steak is an economical cut of beef and is excellent for soups and stews. In this recipe, the beefy flavor is enhanced with red wine and green peppers which are generally plentiful at this time of year.

¹/₂ cup	unsalted butter	125 mL
2 lb	flank steak, diced in ¹/₂-inch (1-cm) cubes	900 g
2 cups	diced Spanish onion	500 mL
3 cups	diced green pepper (about 3 medium)	750 mL
¹/₂ cup	diced carrots (about 1 medium)	125 mL
1 tsp	minced garlic	5 mL
¹/₂ tsp	dried tarragon	2 mL
¹/₂ cup	dry red wine	125 mL
¹/₄ cup	hard or all-purpose flour	50 mL
8 cups	beef stock	2 L
2 tbsp	tomato paste	30 mL
3 tbsp	chili sauce	45 mL
1 tsp	Dijon mustard	5 mL
	salt to taste	
	black pepper to taste	

In a large soup pot, melt $1/4$ cup of butter over medium-high heat until foamy. Add beef and sauté about 3 or 4 minutes, stirring occasionally until lightly browned. Add onion, green pepper, carrots, garlic, and tarragon and continue to sauté, stirring frequently, 3 or 4 minutes more, or until onion has wilted. Stir in red wine, bring to a boil, and reduce to half the amount. Remove to a bowl and set aside.

Add the remaining butter to soup pot and melt over medium-high heat. Then stir in flour and continue to cook, stirring constantly, until the flour is golden brown, about 3 or 4 minutes. While whisking constantly, pour in $1/2$ cup (125 mL) of stock at a time until the mixture is smooth and has thickened slightly. Whisk in tomato paste, chili sauce, and mustard. Bring to a boil, reduce heat to medium-low, add vegetable/meat mixture, and simmer for 5 or 10 minutes or until vegetables are tender. Season with salt and pepper and serve.

SERVES 10 TO 12.

SICILIAN MEATBALL SOUP

Another Italian confection to spice up a cool fall day.

MEATBALLS

½ lb	ground beef	225 g
½ tsp	ground black pepper	2 mL
½ tsp	salt	2 mL
1 tsp	Worcestershire sauce	5 mL
½ tsp	minced garlic	2 mL
1	egg, slightly beaten	1
2 tbsp	chopped parsley	30 mL
¼ cup	vegetable oil	50 mL

SOUP

¼ cup	unsalted butter	50 mL
1½ cups	diced Spanish onions	375 mL
1 cup	diced green peppers	250 mL
½ cup	finely diced celery	125 mL
½ cup	finely diced leek	125 mL
½ tsp	minced garlic	2 mL
½ tsp	fennel seeds	2 mL
½ tsp	dried oregano	2 mL
10	large tomatoes, peeled, seeded, and chopped	10
2 cups	beef stock	500 mL
	salt to taste	
	black pepper to taste	

For meatballs, combine beef, pepper, salt, Worcestershire sauce, garlic, egg, and parsley. Work by hand until thoroughly mixed. Roll into 1-inch (2-cm) diameter meatballs. There should be about 15 to 20 meatballs.

In a large skillet, heat oil over medium-high heat. Add meatballs and brown on all sides.

In a medium-sized, heavy soup pot, heat butter over medium-high heat until melted. Add onions, peppers, celery, leek, and garlic, and sauté for 3 to 4 minutes, stirring occasionally until the vegetables are wilted. Add fennel, oregano, tomatoes, and stock, and simmer for 15 minutes. Add meatballs, season with salt and pepper, and serve.

SERVES 8 TO 10.

ITALIAN SAUSAGE SOUP

*A hearty, Italian-flavored meal-in-a-bowl, this spicy
autumn soup makes good family fare.*

1/4 cup	unsalted butter	50 mL
2 cups	finely diced leeks	500 mL
1 cup	finely diced onion	250 mL
1 cup	finely diced celery	250 mL
1 cup	diced green pepper (about 1 pepper)	250 mL
1 tsp	minced garlic	5 mL
8 cups	tomatoes, peeled, seeded, and diced (about 8 large)	2 L
1/2 tsp	oregano	2 mL
1/2 tsp	fennel seeds	2 mL
1 tbsp	granulated sugar	15 mL
1	dried chili pepper, crushed	1
2 cups	chicken stock	500 mL
2 tbsp	tomato paste	30 mL
3/4 lb	Italian sausage	350 g
1 tsp	Worcestershire sauce	5 mL
	salt to taste	
	white pepper to taste	

In a large, heavy soup pot, melt butter over medium-high heat. Add leeks, onions, celery, green pepper, and garlic; sweat until vegetables are tender, about 4 to 5 minutes. Add tomatoes, oregano, fennel seeds, and sugar, and simmer for 20 minutes. Stir in chili pepper, chicken stock, tomato paste, and sausages, and continue to cook for 10 to 15 minutes or until sausages are fully cooked. Remove sausages to a plate and allow to cool, cut into 1-inch (2-cm) slices and return to soup pot. Season with Worcestershire sauce, salt, and pepper and serve.

SERVES 8 TO 10.

RABBIT BOURGUIGNONNE

*Meaty and satisfying and rich with red wine, this robust
soup from Burgundy turns any dinner into a feast.*

2 cups	dried Black Forest mushrooms	500 mL
2 cups	boiling water	500 mL
1/3 cup	unsalted butter	75 mL
1/3 cup	all-purpose or hard flour	75 mL
1 3-lb	rabbit, cut into 8 pieces	1 1.3-kg
2 cups	diced Spanish onion (about 1 large)	500 mL
1 cup	diced green pepper (about 1 large)	250 mL
1 tbsp	minced garlic (about 3 medium)	15 mL
30	juniper berries	30
1/2 tsp	dried tarragon	2 mL
1/4 cup	tomato paste	50 mL
3/4 cup	black currant jelly or jam	175 mL
2 cups	dry red wine	500 mL
8 cups	demiglace	2 L
1 tbsp	Worcestershire sauce	15 mL
	salt to taste	
	white pepper to taste	

Cover mushrooms with water and soak until soft, about 1 hour. Remove end tips and slice. Reserve liquid.

Preheat oven to 450°F (250°C). In a large, heavy soup pot, heat butter over high heat until bubbly. Meanwhile, place flour in a plastic bag. Add 1 or 2 pieces of rabbit to plastic bag and shake until coated. Sauté until golden brown, about 3 minutes each side, and remove to a platter. Add onion and green pepper and brown, stirring frequently, about 3 to 4 minutes. Add garlic, juniper berries, tarragon, and mushrooms, and continue cooking for 2 or 3 minutes. Stir in tomato paste and cook for 1 minute, stirring constantly. Stir in jelly until melted. Then stir in wine, bring to a boil, and reduce by half. Stir in demiglace and mushroom liquid. Bring to a boil, cover, and bake in preheated oven for 40 minutes or until rabbit is tender. Remove rabbit to a platter and allow to cool, then pick meat off bones, chop coarsely, and return to soup. Season with Worcestershire sauce, salt, and pepper. Heat through and serve.

SERVES 10 TO 12.

QUAIL PERIGORDINE
WITH TRUFFLES

*For very special occasions, there are very few soups that
will speak as subtly and yet convincingly of your
culinary skills as this delicious autumn concoction.*

¹/₄ cup	unsalted butter	50 mL
5 tbsp	hard or all-purpose flour	75 mL
3 tbsp	unsalted butter	45 mL
3	medium quail, each cut into 4 pieces	3
1 cup	finely diced Spanish onions	250 mL
¹/₂ cup	sliced mushrooms	125 mL
¹/₄ cup	finely diced shallots	50 mL
¹/₂ tsp	minced garlic	2 mL
¹/₄ oz	truffles	5 g
¹/₄ cup	cognac	50 mL
2¹/₂ oz	pate de foie gras	75 g
1 cup	dry red wine	250 mL
8 cups	chicken stock	2 L
¹/₃ cup	whipping cream (35 percent)	75 mL
	salt to taste	
	black pepper to taste	

In a medium-sized, heavy soup pot, heat 2 tbsp of the butter over high heat until bubbly. Meanwhile, place 2 tbsp of the flour in a plastic bag; put 1 or 2 pieces of quail in the bag, and shake until pieces are coated with flour. Sauté quail until golden brown, about 3 minutes each side, and remove to a platter. Reduce heat to medium-high. Add 1 tbsp of butter, onions, mushrooms, shallots, garlic, and truffles, and sauté until golden brown, about 6 or 7 minutes. Return quail to pot. Stir in cognac and ignite with a match to flambé. Once flames die out completely, whisk in pâté. Stir in wine, bring to a boil, and reduce to half the amount. Add stock, bring to a boil, reduce heat to medium-low, and simmer for 20 minutes, or until soup is reduced by about one third. With a slotted spoon, remove quail to a plate to cool. Once it is cool, remove the meat from the bones, discarding the bones, and return the meat to the pot.

In a separate heavy soup pot, heat the remaining butter over medium-high heat until melted. Whisk in remaining flour and cook for 5 to 7 minutes, whisking constantly until medium brown color. Slowly whisk in $1/2$ cup of soup mixture at a time until mixture is smooth.

Stir in cream and season with salt and pepper. Bring to a boil and serve.

SERVES 2 TO 4.

THICK DUCK
WITH MORELS AND BURGUNDY

*This is a filling, spicy soup
perfect for the cooler days of autumn.*

STOCK

3.3 lbs	duck	1.5 kg
12 cups	cold water	3 L
2	medium carrots, chopped	2
1	medium onion with its skin	1
1	leek, chopped	1
½ tsp	dried thyme	2 mL
2	bay leaves	2

SOUP

1½ cups	dried morels	375 mL
2½ cups	boiling water	625 mL
1¼ cups	unsalted butter	300 mL
3 cups	diced Spanish onion (about 2 onions)	750 mL
2 cups	diced leeks (about 2 medium leeks)	500 mL
½ cup	diced pimento or red pepper (about ½ a pepper)	125 mL
½ tsp	dried tarragon	2 mL
1 tsp	dried rosemary	5 mL
3	juniper berries	3

1 tbsp	brown or demerara sugar	15 mL
1 tbsp	tomato paste	15 mL
1 tsp	minced garlic (1 large clove)	5 mL
1 cup	dry red wine	250 mL
1 cup	hard white flour	250 mL
9 cups	duck stock	2.25 L
¼ cup	port	50 mL
¼ cup	whipping cream (35 percent)	50 mL
¼ tsp	ground mace	1 mL
	salt to taste	
	white pepper to taste	

Preheat oven to 450°F (250°C).

To make duck stock, debone duck, dice meat, and set aside for the soup; discard skin. Break up bones and place them in a shallow roasting pan. Roast in preheated oven until dark brown, about 1 hour, turning once or twice. Combine browned bones, water, carrots, onion, leek, thyme, and bay leaves in a large stock pot. Bring to a boil over medium-high heat. Reduce heat to medium-low and simmer 1 or 2 hours, skimming off the foam as it appears and adding more water as necessary to keep the level constant. This process should yield about 10 to 12 cups of duck stock.

Meanwhile, cover the morels with boiling water and allow them to soften (about 20 minutes). Once softened, remove the ends of the stems and slice each mushroom in half. Reserve 2 cups of the mushroom liquid for the soup.

In a large, heavy soup pot, melt ¼ cup of the butter over high heat until foamy. Add duck meat and brown, cooking about 4 minutes, stirring occasionally. Reduce heat to medium-high, add onions, leeks, and pimento, and continue to cook until onion is transparent, about 3 minutes. Stir in tarragon, rosemary, juniper berries, sugar, tomato paste, and garlic, and continue to cook 1 minute, stirring constantly. Stir in red wine, bring to a boil, and reduce until almost gone. Add morel liquid and set entire mixture aside.

In a large, heavy soup pot, melt remaining butter over medium-high heat. Once melted, whisk in flour and continue to cook until golden brown, whisking constantly, about 5 minutes. While whisking continuously, pour in $1/2$ cup of stock at a time until smooth and thick. Stir in port, duck/vegetable mixture, and cream, and season with mace, salt, and pepper. Bring to a boil and serve.

SERVES 10 TO 12.

OYSTER STEW

This is a delightful version of the well-known stew from Canada's Maritime provinces.

2 tbsp	unsalted butter	30 mL
½ cup	finely diced onion	125 mL
½ cup	finely diced leek	125 mL
½ tsp	minced garlic	2 mL
12	fresh oysters, shucked, reserve juice	12
1 tbsp	brandy	15 mL
2 tbsp	dry white wine	30 mL
1½ cups	whipping cream (35 percent)	375 mL
½ tsp	Worcestershire sauce	2 mL
	ground nutmeg to taste	
	salt to taste	
	white pepper to taste	
1 tbsp	grated cheese	15 mL

Heat butter in a medium-sized, heavy saucepan over medium-high heat. Add onion, leek, and garlic; sweat until onion is transparent and leek is tender, about 3 or 4 minutes. Add oysters, oyster juice, and brandy. As soon as brandy is warm, ignite with a match to flambé. Once flames have died out completely, stir in wine and bring mixture just to a boil. Stir in cream and season with Worcestershire sauce, nutmeg, salt, and pepper. Stir in cheese and serve,

SERVES 2.

FROG VELOUTÉ

The French call them grenouilles, *and for those who swoon at the mention of frogs' legs, this creamy dinner soup is simply* magnifique!

¹⁄₄ cup	unsalted butter	50 mL
1¹⁄₄ lbs	frogs' legs	575 g
2 cups	diced Spanish onion	500 mL
2 cups	diced leeks (about 2 leeks)	500 mL
4	juniper berries	4
1 tsp	minced garlic (about 1 large)	5 mL
¹⁄₂ tsp	dried tarragon	2 mL
¹⁄₂ cup	dry white wine	125 mL
¹⁄₄ cup	dry sherry	50 mL
9 cups	chicken stock	2.25 L
5 tbsp	beurre-manié	75 mL
1 cup	whipping cream (35 percent)	250 mL
¹⁄₂ tsp	ground nutmeg	2 mL
¹⁄₂ tsp	Worcestershire sauce	2 mL
	salt to taste	
	white pepper to taste	

In a large, heavy soup pot, melt butter over high heat until nutty brown color. Add frogs' legs and fry until golden brown, turning once. Reduce heat to medium-high; add onion, leeks, and juniper berries and continue to cook about 3 minutes, stirring constantly or until vegetables are wilted. Add garlic and tarragon and cook 30 seconds more. Stir in wine and sherry, bring to a boil, and reduce by half. Add stock, return to a boil, reduce heat to medium-low, and simmer 10 minutes or more, or until meat pulls away easily from the bone. Remove frogs' legs to a platter and allow to cool enough to pick off meat; dice meat and set aside.

Bring soup back to a boil over medium-high heat. In a medium-sized bowl, whisk beurre-manié until smooth. Slowly whisk in 1 cup (250 mL) of the soup mixture until beurre-manié resembles a smooth paste. Whisk into the soup a spoonful at a time. Simmer 2 to 3 minutes or until soup thickens slightly.

Return frog meat to soup. Stir in cream and season with nutmeg, Worcestershire sauce, salt, and pepper. Bring to a boil and serve.

SERVES 8 TO 10.

BLACK FOREST MUSHROOM
WITH RED WINE

One taste of these chewy, sweet, flavorful mushrooms, and you will understand why they are among the most coveted types of mushroom. And one sip of this hearty, smooth, and delicious soup will convince you that no kitchen should be without a good supply of dried mushrooms on hand.

4 cups	dried Black Forest mushrooms	1 L
4 cups	boiling water	1 L
1/4 cup	unsalted butter	50 mL
2 cups	diced Spanish onion (about 1 large)	500 mL
1 cup	diced leek (about 1 large)	250 mL
1 cup	finely diced green pepper	250 mL
1 1/2 tsp	minced garlic (about 2 medium)	7 mL
1 tsp	dried tarragon	5 mL
1/2 cup	red wine	125 mL
8 cups	chicken stock	2 L
5 tbsp	beurre-manié	75 mL
1 cup	whipping cream (35 percent)	250 mL
1 tsp	Worcestershire sauce	5 mL
1/2 tsp	ground nutmeg	2 mL
	salt to taste	
	white pepper to taste	

In a medium-sized bowl, cover mushrooms with boiling water, allow to sit about 2 hours or until mushrooms have softened. Remove ends of mushroom stems and slice. Reserve liquid.

In a large, heavy soup pot, heat butter over medium-high heat until butter begins to turn a nutty brown color. Add onion, leek, and pepper; sweat 3 to 4 minutes or until softened. Add garlic and mushrooms and sauté for 3 to 4 minutes. Add tarragon, red wine, chicken stock, and mushroom liquid. Bring to a boil, reduce heat to medium, and simmer for 10 minutes or until mushrooms have softened.

In a medium-sized bowl, whisk beurre-manié until smooth. Slowly whisk in 1 cup (250 mL) of the soup mixture until beurre-manié resembles a smooth paste. Add to the soup 1 spoonful at a time, whisking constantly. Simmer until thickened slightly.

Stir in cream and season with Worcestershire sauce, nutmeg, salt, and pepper. Bring back to a boil and serve.

SERVES 8 TO 10.

STRACCIATELLA

*Vegetables and pasta in splendid combination, a
delightful and nutritious addition to any fall menu.*

¼ cup	unsalted butter	50 mL
2 cups	chopped onion (about 1 large)	500 mL
1 cup	sliced leek (about 1 large)	250 mL
½ tsp	minced garlic	2 mL
1 cup	finely sliced carrots (about 2 medium)	250 mL
1 cup	sliced mushrooms	250 mL
3 cups	sliced zucchini (about 3 small)	750 mL
1	head of broccoli, coarsely chopped	1
1 cup	diced green pepper (about 1 medium)	250 mL
3 cups	tomatoes, diced (about 3 medium)	750 mL
1 tbsp	dried oregano	15 mL
7 cups	chicken stock	1.75 L
3 oz	vermicelli noodles, broken into 2-inch (5-cm) lengths	85 g
2	large eggs, beaten	2
1 cup	grated parmesan cheese	250 mL
1¼ cups	lemon juice (juice of 1½ lemons)	50 mL
1 tsp	Worcestershire sauce	5 mL
	salt to taste	
	white pepper to taste	

In a large, heavy soup pot, melt butter over medium-high heat. When butter begins to foam, add onion and leek; sauté 3 to 4 minutes or until vegetables have wilted. Add garlic and sauté for 1 minute, stirring constantly. Add carrots, mushrooms, zucchini, broccoli, green pepper, tomatoes, and oregano. Sauté for 10 minutes, but do not brown. Stir in stock. Bring to a boil, reduce heat to medium and simmer for 15 minutes or until vegetables are tender. Add noodles and continue to simmer for 10 minutes.

In a medium-sized bowl, beat eggs with a fork until frothy. Bring soup to a rolling boil, and slowly add eggs to soup while mixing soup continuously. Then add spoonfuls of cheese to soup while mixing continuously. Season with lemon juice, Worcestershire sauce, salt, and pepper.

SERVES 10 TO 12.

CARIBBEAN PEPPER POT

A peppery tribute to the Caribbean, guaranteed to wake up your taste buds and add spice to a brisk autumn day.

1/3 cup	unsalted butter	75 mL
2 cups	finely diced green bell peppers (about 2 medium)	500 mL
1 cup	finely diced sweet red pepper (about 1 medium)	250 mL
1 cup	finely diced Spanish onion	250 mL
1 tbsp	dried red peppercorns	15 mL
6	black peppercorns	6
1/4 cup	ground Spanish paprika	50 mL
1/2 tsp	minced garlic	2 mL
2 tbsp	dry white wine	30 mL
3 tbsp	white vinegar	45 mL
2 tbsp	green peppercorns	30 mL
2 tbsp	brine from green peppercorns	30 mL
1 tbsp	granulated sugar	15 mL
9 cups	chicken stock	2.25 L
8 tbsp	beurre-manié	120 mL
1/2 cup	whipping cream (35 percent)	125 mL
1 tsp	dry mustard	5 mL
	ground nutmeg to taste	
	salt to taste	
	white pepper to taste	

In a large, heavy soup pot, melt butter over medium-high heat. When butter begins to foam slightly, add green and red peppers, onions, and red and black peppercorns and sauté 3 or 4 minutes or until onions have wilted slightly. Stir in paprika and garlic and continue to cook 1 or 2 minutes while stirring constantly, so as not to burn the paprika. Stir in wine and vinegar and reduce by half the amount. Add green peppercorns, brine, sugar, and stock. Bring to a boil, reduce heat to medium, and simmer for 10 minutes.

In a medium-sized bowl, whisk beurre-manié until smooth. Slowly whisk in 1 to 2 cups (250 to 500 mL) of the soup mixture until beurre-manié resembles a smooth paste. Whisk into the soup a spoonful at a time, whisking constantly. Simmer gently to thicken slightly.

Stir in cream and season with mustard, nutmeg, salt, and pepper. Bring to a boil and serve piping hot.

SERVES 7 TO 9.

CREAM OF
ZUCCHINI
AND EGGPLANT

*For those who prefer creamed soups, this healthful,
easy-to-make, and delicious soup will become
an instant favorite.*

¹/₄ cup	unsalted butter	50 mL
1 cup	finely diced leeks	250 mL
1 cup	finely diced onions	250 mL
2 cups	diced zucchini	500 mL
2 cups	unpeeled, diced eggplant	500 mL
¹/₄ cup	finely diced sweet red pepper or pimento	50 mL
1 tsp	minced garlic (about 1 medium clove)	5 mL
¹/₂ tsp	dried tarragon	2 mL
¹/₂ tsp	chopped fresh basil	2 mL
¹/₄ cup	dry white wine	50 mL
8 cups	chicken stock	2 L
6 tbsp	beurre-manié	90 mL
¹/₂ cup	whipping cream (35 percent)	125 mL
1 tsp	Worcestershire sauce	5 mL
	ground nutmeg to taste	
	salt to taste	
	white pepper to taste	

In a large, heavy soup pot, melt butter over medium-high heat until butter turns to a nutty brown color. Add leeks, onions, zucchini, eggplant, red pepper, and garlic; sweat until vegetables are tender, about 5 minutes.

Stir in tarragon, basil, and wine, bring to a boil, and reduce by half, about 2 to 3 minutes. Stir in stock, bring to a boil, reduce heat to medium, and simmer for 5 minutes.

In a medium-sized bowl, whisk beurre-manié until smooth. Slowly whisk in 1 to 2 cups (250 to 500 mL) of the soup mixture until beurre-manié resembles a smooth paste. Whisk into the soup 1 spoonful at a time, whisking constantly. Simmer until soup has thickened slightly.

Bring soup back to a boil, stir in cream, and season with Worcestershire sauce, nutmeg, salt, and pepper. Serve immediately.

SERVES 8 TO 10.

PHEASANT AND CHANTERELLES
WITH BEAUJOLAIS

Autumn appetites will be more than satisfied with this tribute to the woodlands.

STOCK

1 3-lb	pheasant	1 1.3-kg
1	medium Spanish onion with its skin, cut into 8 pieces	1
3	garlic cloves in their skin	3
2	medium carrots, coarsely chopped	2
2	medium stalks of celery, coarsely chopped	2
12 cups	cold water	3 L
1 tbsp	tomato paste	15 mL
1 tsp	dried thyme	5 mL
1 tsp	dried tarragon	5 mL
6	peppercorns	6
2	bay leaves	2

SOUP

1¼ cups	unsalted butter	300 mL
1 cup	diced Spanish onion	250 mL
1 cup	diced leek (about 1 large)	250 mL
1 tsp	minced garlic (about 1 large)	5 mL

1 tsp	dried thyme	5 mL
1 tsp	dried tarragon	5 mL
2 cups	fresh chanterelle mushrooms, sliced	500 mL
1/4 cup	port	50 mL
1 cup	Beaujolais	250 mL
1 cup	hard white flour	250 mL
10 cups	pheasant stock	2.5 L
2 tbsp	whipping cream (35 percent)	30 mL
1 tsp	Worcestershire sauce	5 mL
	salt to taste	
	white pepper to taste	

Preheat oven to 450°F (250°C).

To make pheasant stock, debone pheasant, dice meat, and set aside for the soup; discard skin. Break up bones and place them in a shallow roasting pan. Roast in preheated oven until bones begin to brown, about 20 minutes. Add onion, garlic, carrots, and celery and continue to cook about 40 minutes or until bones and vegetables turn dark brown. Combine browned bones and vegetables with water, tomato paste, thyme, tarragon, peppercorns, and bay leaves in a large stock pot. Bring to a boil over medium-high heat. Reduce heat to medium-low and simmer 1 to 2 hours, skimming off the foam as it appears, and adding more water as necessary to keep the level constant. This process should yield 10 to 12 cups of pheasant stock.

In a large, heavy soup pot, melt 1/4 cup of the butter over high heat until foamy. Add pheasant meat and sauté about 4 minutes, stirring occasionally, until meat is brown. With a slotted spoon, remove meat to a medium-sized bowl. Reduce heat to medium-high, add onion and leek and brown vegetables, stirring frequently. Add garlic, thyme, tarragon, and chanterelles. Sweat 2 to 3 minutes, stirring occasionally until mushrooms are tender. Stir in port and Beaujolais, bring to a boil, and reduce by half. Remove all ingredients to bowl with pheasant meat.

Add the remaining butter to the soup pot and melt over medium-high heat. Once melted, whisk in flour and continue to cook until golden brown, whisking constantly, about 4 to 5 minutes. While whisking constantly, pour in $1/2$ cup (125 mL) stock at a time, until mixture is smooth and thick. Stir in vegetable/meat mixture and cream. Season with Worcestershire sauce, salt, and pepper. Bring to a boil and serve.

SERVES 10 TO 12.

WINTER

WINTER

Full knee-deep lies the winter snow,
And the winter winds are wearily sighing.

Tennyson

If there is a soup season, a genuine steaming pot and meal-in-a-bowl time of year, this is it. The Christmas and New Year's holidays are marked with celebration and feasting, and giant-sized appetites hover about the table, if not the kitchen itself. The tradition, it seems, has always been with us. In the olden days, when stock pots simmered unattended on stove tops and creative cooking meant adding a little of this, a little of that, the rich, fragrant, welcoming aroma of homemade soup was as much a part of winter as hats, mittens, and frozen toes.

Not much has changed. Soup is still the most warming and wholesome winter fare, and although stock pots have been largely replaced by food processors and electric crock pots, the very best soups of all are made from homemade stock.

Here, then, is a selection of soup recipes for all winter occasions—from après-ski (or after school) to elegant entertaining (or the sudden arrival of unexpected but welcome company).

THICK LAMB

This is definitely a meal-in-a-bowl type of soup. Rich, savory, and satisfying, this is one for chalet country. Serve it at an après-ski get-together.

STOCK

3 lbs	lamb (shank and neck bones)	1.3 kg
1	medium onion, with skin	1
2	medium carrots, coarsely chopped	2
2	celery stalks, coarsely chopped	2
2	cloves garlic, with skin	2
12 cups	cold water	3 L
2 tbsp	tomato paste	30 mL
1/2 tsp	dried thyme	2 mL
1/4 tsp	dried rosemary	1 mL
8	black peppercorns	8
2	bay leaves	2

SOUP

1/2 cup + 1 tbsp	unsalted butter	140 mL
1 lb	coarsely ground lamb	450 g
1 cup	diced Spanish onion	250 mL
1 cup	diced leek	250 mL
1/4 cup	diced green pepper	50 mL
1 tsp	minced garlic	5 mL

½ tsp	dried thyme	2 mL
½ tsp	dried rosemary	2 mL
1 tbsp	tomato paste	15 mL
¼ cup	chili sauce	50 mL
¼ cup	dry red wine	50 mL
8 cups	lamb stock	2 L
⅓ cup	hard or all-purpose flour	75 mL
	salt to taste	
	black pepper to taste	

Preheat oven to 450°F (250°C).

To make lamb stock, place bones in a shallow roasting pan and roast in preheated oven until they begin to brown, about 30 minutes. Add onion, carrots, celery, and garlic and continue to cook about 30 minutes more or until bones and vegetables are a dark brown color. Combine browned bones and vegetables, water, tomato paste, thyme, rosemary, peppercorns, and bay leaves in a large stock pot. Bring to a boil over medium-high heat. Reduce heat to medium-low and simmer for 1 or 2 hours, skimming off the foam as it appears and adding more water as necessary to keep the level constant. Strain the stock, discarding the bones and vegetables. Bring back to a boil and reduce by a quarter to about 8 cups of strong stock.

In a large, heavy soup pot, melt ¼ cup of butter over medium-high heat. Add lamb and sauté for 4 or 5 minutes, stirring occasionally until browned. Add onion, leek, green pepper, garlic, thyme, and rosemary, and sauté for 5 to 6 minutes, or until vegetables begin to brown. Stir in tomato paste, chili sauce, and wine. Bring to a boil, then add the stock. Bring back to a boil, reduce heat to medium-low, and simmer for 20 to 25 minutes.

In another large, heavy soup pot, melt remaining butter over medium-high heat. Then whisk in flour and continue to cook, whisking constantly, until mixture is golden brown, about 4 or 5 minutes. While whisking, pour in $1/2$ cup of soup mixture at a time until smooth. Simmer until thickened slightly, about 5 or 6 minutes. Season with salt and pepper and serve.

SERVES 5 TO 7.

OXTAIL SOUP

Anyone buying oxtails for the first time can be forgiven
for wondering how beef bones with so little meat on
them could possibly produce a soup as flavorful as this.
Tasting is believing!

STOCK

1 lb	oxtail bones	450 g
1	medium carrot, coarsely chopped	1
1	medium stalk celery, coarsely chopped	1
1	medium onion, quartered	1
3	garlic cloves	3
1 tbsp	tomato paste	15 mL
12 cups	cold water	3 L
1 tsp	dried thyme	5 mL
2	bay leaves	2

SOUP

¼ cup	unsalted butter	50 mL
2 cups	diced leeks	500 mL
1 cup	diced Spanish onion	250 mL
½ cup	diced carrots	125 mL
¼ tsp	minced garlic	1 mL
¼ tsp	dried tarragon	1 mL

1 tbsp	tomato paste	15 mL
½ cup	dry red wine	125 mL
10 cups	oxtail stock	2.5 L
3 tbsp	beurre-manié	45 mL
1 dash	Worcestershire sauce	1
	salt to taste	
	white pepper to taste	

Preheat oven to 450°F (250°C).

To make oxtail stock, place bones in a shallow roasting pan and roast in preheated oven until they begin to brown, about 20 minutes. Turn bones and add carrot, celery, onion, garlic, and tomato paste, and continue to roast for 40 minutes. Combine browned bones and vegetables with water, thyme, and bay leaves in a large stock pot. Bring to a boil over medium-high heat. Reduce heat to medium-low and simmer for 1 to 2 hours, skimming off the foam as it appears and adding more water as necessary to keep the level constant. This process should yield 10 to 12 cups of oxtail stock.

In a large, heavy soup pot, melt butter over medium-high heat until it turns a light nutty brown color. Add leeks, onions, carrots, and garlic; sweat for 3 or 4 minutes or until vegetables wilt slightly. Add tarragon and tomato paste and continue to cook for 3 to 4 minutes, stirring occasionally. Stir in wine, bring to a boil, and reduce to half the amount. Stir in stock, return to boil, reduce heat to medium-low, and simmer for 15 to 20 minutes or until reduced by about a quarter. Remove oxtail bones to a plate to cool. When they are cool, remove the meat from the bones, discard the bones, and return the meat to the soup mixture.

In a medium-sized bowl, whisk beurre-manié until smooth. Slowly whisk in 1 cup (250 mL) of the soup mixture until beurre-manié resembles a smooth paste. Whisk into the soup mixture 1 spoonful at a time. Simmer gently to thicken slightly.

Season with Worcestershire sauce, salt, and pepper and serve.

SERVES 10 TO 12.

CHICKEN BASMATI

*It's rare to find someone who doesn't like chicken soup.
Here's an excellent variation on traditional
chicken-with-rice soup that will have family and friends
calling for seconds.*

¹/₄ cup	unsalted butter	50 mL
2 3-oz	boned, skinned chicken breasts, diced into ¹/₂-inch (1-cm) cubes	2 85-g
1 cup	diced Spanish onion	250 mL
¹/₄ cup	diced leek	50 mL
¹/₄ cup	diced green pepper	50 mL
¹/₄ cup	diced celery	50 mL
¹/₃ cup	basmati rice	75 mL
1 tsp	minced garlic	5 mL
¹/₂ tsp	dried oregano	2 mL
2	tomatoes, diced	2
8 cups	chicken stock	2 L
	salt to taste	
	white pepper to taste	

In a large, heavy soup pot, melt butter over medium-high heat until foamy. Add chicken, onion, leek, green pepper, and celery, and sauté stirring frequently, for 5 minutes, or until chicken turns opaque and vegetables wilt slightly. Add rice, garlic, oregano, and tomatoes, and continue to sauté for 2 minutes, stirring constantly. Stir in stock, bring to a boil, reduce heat to medium-low, and simmer for 12 to 15 minutes, or until rice is completely cooked.

Season with salt and pepper and serve.

SERVES 6 TO 8.

CHICKEN NOODLE

This thick and hearty version of an age-old standard will give a whole new meaning to the words "chicken noodle soup."

¹/₄ cup	unsalted butter	50 mL
2 cups	diced onions	500 mL
2 cups	diced leeks	500 mL
1 cup	diced carrots	250 mL
1¹/₂ cups	diced celery	375 mL
¹/₂ cup	sliced mushrooms	125 mL
¹/₄ cup	finely diced sweet red pepper or pimento	50 mL
2 tsp	minced garlic	10 mL
3 oz	fettucine noodles, in 1-inch (2-cm) pieces	85 g
12 cups	chicken stock	3 L
3 cups	diced chicken (about 3 breasts)	750 mL
1 tbsp	Worcestershire sauce	15 mL
2 tbsp	finely diced parsley	30 mL
	salt to taste	
	white pepper to taste	

In a large soup pot, melt butter over medium-high heat until bubbling. Add onions, leeks, carrots, celery, mushrooms, and red pepper. Cook until vegetables are wilted, about 6 or 7 minutes, stirring occasionally. Add garlic and noodles and continue to cook, stirring frequently, for 5 to 6 minutes, or until noodles are slightly sautéed. Stir in stock and chicken, bring to a boil, reduce heat to medium-low, and simmer for 20 to 25 minutes, or until chicken and noodles are completely cooked. Season with Worcestershire sauce, parsley, salt, and pepper and serve.

SERVES 12 TO 14.

CRABMEAT RAREBIT
WITH BEER

Tender chunks of delicious crabmeat and the addition of beer make this rarebit a rare treat on a winter's eve. Thick and creamy and entirely satisfying!

10 cups	2 percent or homogenized milk	2.5 L
1 cup	unsalted butter	250 mL
3 cups	diced Spanish onion	750 mL
½ cup	diced pimento or sweet red pepper	125 mL
1¼ cups	hard or all-purpose flour	300 mL
1½ lbs	snow crabmeat	675 g
½ cup	warm, flat beer	125 mL
½ tsp	dried tarragon	2 mL
1 tsp	dried mustard	5 mL
1 tsp	Worcestershire sauce	5 mL
1½ lb	grated aged cheddar cheese	675 g
1 cup	whipping cream (35 percent)	250 mL
½ tsp	ground nutmeg	2 mL
	salt to taste	
	white pepper to taste	

Bring milk just to a boil in a large soup pot over medium-high heat.

Meanwhile, in another large, heavy soup pot, melt butter over medium-high heat. Add onion and pimento and cook until they are wilted, about 3 minutes. Whisk in flour and continue to cook another 2 to 3 minutes, whisking constantly so as not to brown. Slowly whisk in $\frac{1}{2}$ cup of milk at a time until mixture is smooth. Simmer until thickened slightly. Stir in crabmeat, beer, tarragon, mustard, and Worcestershire sauce. While whisking constantly, add a handful of cheese at a time until cheese has completely melted. Stir in cream and season with nutmeg, salt, and pepper. Bring to a boil and ladle into soup bowls.

SERVES 14 TO 16.

SCALLOP MORNAY

A creamy, cheese-flavored soup that takes its inspiration from the sea. Scallops can be bought fresh or frozen throughout the year.

¼ cup	unsalted butter	50 mL
1 cup	finely diced Spanish onion	250 mL
½ lb	scallop pieces	225 g
1 tsp	minced garlic	5 mL
¼ cup	diced pimento or sweet red pepper	50 mL
1 tsp	dried tarragon	5 mL
½ cup	dry white wine	125 mL
¼ cup	cognac	50 mL
7 cups	chicken stock	1.75 L
5 tbsp	beurre-manié	75 mL
½ lb	grated Swiss or gruyère cheese	225 g
1 cup	whipping cream (35 percent)	250 mL
½ tsp	ground nutmeg	2 mL
1 tbsp	dry mustard	15 mL
	salt to taste	
	white pepper to taste	

In a large, heavy soup pot, melt butter over medium-high heat. Add onion, scallops, and garlic, and sauté until onion is translucent but not browned, about 5 minutes. Add pimento and tarragon and continue to cook for 3 minutes or until pimento has softened. Stir in wine, cognac, and chicken stock. Bring to a boil, then reduce heat to medium and simmer for 5 to 10 minutes.

In a medium-sized bowl, whisk beurre-manié until smooth. Slowly whisk in 1 cup (250 mL) of the soup mixture until beurre-manié resembles a smooth paste. Add to the soup 1 spoonful at a time, stirring constantly. Simmer gently to thicken slightly.

Add cheese to the soup a handful at a time, stirring constantly until melted. Stir in cream and season with nutmeg, mustard, salt, and pepper. Serve steaming hot.

SERVES 8 TO 10.

SHRIMP BISQUE

A romantic dinner for two, or an elegant dinner party for special friends can be made extra-special with this aromatic favorite.

STOCK

1 lb	jumbo shrimps, shelled, cleaned, and halved lengthwise (keep shells for stock)	450 g
8 cups	chicken stock or water	2 L
1	onion, quartered	1
2	bay leaves	2

SOUP

¼ cup	unsalted butter	50 mL
1 cup	finely diced shallots	250 mL
2 cups	sliced mushrooms	500 mL
¼ cup	finely diced sweet red pepper or pimento	50 mL
1 tsp	minced garlic	5 mL
½ tsp	dried tarragon	2 mL
⅓ cup	cognac	75 mL
1 tbsp	sherry	15 mL
2 tbsp	dry white wine	30 mL
7 cups	shrimp stock	1.75 L
8 tbsp	beurre-manié	125 mL

½ cup	whipping cream (35 percent)	125 mL
1 tsp	Worcestershire sauce	5 mL
	pinch of dry mustard	
	ground nutmeg to taste	
	salt to taste	
	white pepper to taste	

To make shrimp stock, combine shrimp shells, chicken stock or water, onion and bay leaves in a medium-sized stock pot. Simmer for 30 to 40 minutes only; fish stock will become bitter if left to simmer longer. Strain and set aside. There should be about 7 cups of stock.

In a large, heavy soup pot, melt butter over medium-high heat. Add shallots, mushrooms, red pepper, and garlic and sauté until shallots have softened, about 3 or 4 minutes, stirring occasionally. Add shrimp and tarragon and continue to sauté until shrimp turn pink, about 3 or 4 minutes. Stir in cognac, ignite with a match, and flambé. Once the flames die out completely, stir in sherry, wine, and shrimp stock.

Bring soup mixture to a boil. Meanwhile, in a medium-sized bowl, whisk beurre-manié until smooth. Slowly whisk in 1 to 2 cups (250 to 500 mL) of the soup mixture until beurre-manié resembles a smooth paste. Whisk into the soup a spoonful at a time, whisking constantly. Simmer until thickened slightly. Stir in cream and season with Worcestershire sauce, mustard, nutmeg, salt, and pepper. Serve immediately.

SERVES 6 TO 8.

CONCH CHOWDER

Tender and spicy, deep red conch chowder has always been a favorite in seafood restaurants and shellfish bars where it is often listed as an alternate to standard East Coast clam chowder. It is similar to Manhattan clam chowder, but spicier.

1 lb	conch meat	450 g
1/3 cup	unsalted butter	75 mL
2 cups	finely diced onion	500 mL
1/2 cup	finely diced leek	125 mL
1 tbsp	finely diced sweet red pepper or pimento	15 mL
1 tbsp	minced garlic (about 3 cloves)	15 mL
1/4 cup	ground Spanish paprika	50 mL
1/2 tsp	dried basil	2 mL
1 tsp	dried tarragon	5 mL
2 tbsp	cognac	30 mL
1/4 cup	dry white wine	50 mL
1/4 cup	dry sherry	50 mL
8 cups	chicken stock	2 L
7 tbsp	beurre-manié	105 mL
1/2 cup	whipping cream (35 percent)	125 mL
1 1/2 tsp	lemon juice (about 1/2 lemon)	7 mL
2 dashes	Worcestershire sauce	2
1/2 tsp	dry mustard	2 mL
	ground nutmeg to taste	
	salt to taste	
	white pepper to taste	

Place conch meat in bowl of food processor fitted with steel blades. Pulse for 1 or 2 minutes until coarsely ground or work through a meat grinder with the largest blade.

In a medium-sized soup pot, melt butter over medium-high heat. When butter begins to foam slightly, add onion, leek, red pepper, and garlic, and sauté 3 to 4 minutes, or until onion wilts slightly. Add conch meat and cook for 2 minutes, while stirring constantly. Stir in paprika, basil, and tarragon and continue to cook for 1 to 2 minutes more. Stir in cognac, ignite with a match, and flambé. When the flames have completely died down, stir in the wine and the sherry. Bring to a boil and reduce by half. Stir in chicken stock. Bring to a boil, reduce heat to medium, and simmer for 10 minutes.

In a medium-sized bowl, whisk beurre-manié until smooth. Slowly whisk in 1 cup (250 mL) of the soup mixture until beurre-manié resembles a smooth paste. Add to the soup 1 spoonful at a time, stirring constantly. Simmer until thickened slightly.

Stir in cream and season with lemon juice, Worcestershire sauce, mustard, nutmeg, salt, and pepper. Serve immediately.

SERVES 6 TO 8.

LEEK AND ENDIVE
IN A CLEAR BROTH

*With leek and endive both in plentiful supply
from October through to May, it's easy to understand
why this delicious soup has become a winter favorite.
This recipe provides a "garden-in-a-bowl" taste
that's hard to beat.*

¹/₄ cup	unsalted butter	50 mL
3 cups	diced leek	750 mL
1 cup	diced onion	250 mL
¹/₂ cup	finely diced sweet red pepper or pimento	125 mL
¹/₂ cup	finely diced green pepper	125 mL
1 cup	sliced mushrooms	250 mL
1 cup	diced celery	250 mL
1 tsp	minced garlic	5 mL
¹/₄ tsp	dried tarragon	1 mL
¹/₂ tsp	dried thyme	2 mL
1¹/₂ tsp	dried oregano	7 mL
¹/₂ tsp	fennel seeds	2 mL
¹/₄ cup	dry sherry	50 mL
1 cup	tomatoes, peeled, seeded, and chopped (about 2 medium)	250 mL
8 cups	chicken stock	2 L
3 cups	sliced Belgian endive (about 3 large)	750 mL
¹/₄ cup	finely chopped garlic dill pickle	50 mL

¹⁄₄ cup	grated parmesan cheese	50 mL
2 tbsp	grated romano cheese	30 mL
	salt to taste	
	white pepper to taste	

In a large soup pot, melt butter over medium-high heat until it turns a light nutty brown color. Add leek, onion, red pepper, green pepper, mushrooms, celery, and garlic; sweat, stirring occasionally, for 3 to 4 minutes, or until vegetables have wilted slightly. Stir in tarragon, thyme, oregano, fennel seeds, and sherry. Add tomatoes and stock, and bring to a boil. Add endive, reduce heat to medium-low, and simmer for 5 minutes.

Stir in pickle and whisk in parmesan and romano cheeses. Season with salt and pepper and serve.

SERVES 10 TO 12.

SCANDINAVIAN POTATO

"If a man really likes potatoes, he must be a pretty decent sort of fellow," said A.A. Milne. This creamy, satisfying winter soup is ideal for pretty hungry sorts of families.

¹⁄₄ cup	unsalted butter	50 mL
4 oz	double smoked pork, cut into ¹⁄₄-inch (0.5-cm) cubes	113 g
1 cup	diced leek	250 mL
1 cup	diced onion	250 mL
¹⁄₄ tsp	minced garlic	1 mL
¹⁄₄ tsp	dried rosemary	1 mL
2 cups	peeled, grated potato (about 3 medium)	500 mL
8 cups	chicken stock	2 L
3 tbsp	beurre-manié	45 mL
¹⁄₂ cup	whipping cream (35 percent)	125 mL
¹⁄₂ tsp	Worcestershire sauce	2 mL
	ground nutmeg to taste	
	salt to taste	
	white pepper to taste	

In a medium-sized, heavy soup pot, melt butter over medium-high heat until it turns a nutty brown color. Add pork and sauté for 1 or 2 minutes, then add leek, onion, garlic, and rosemary and continue to sauté until onion is translucent. Add potato and cook for 2 to 3 minutes, stirring frequently so as not to burn. Stir in stock, bring to a boil, reduce heat to medium, and simmer for 20 minutes.

In a medium-sized bowl, whisk beurre-manié until smooth. Slowly whisk in 1 to 2 cups (250 to 500 mL) of the soup mixture until it resembles a smooth paste. Whisk into the soup mixture 1 spoonful at a time. Simmer gently to thicken slightly.

Stir in cream and season with Worcestershire sauce, nutmeg, salt, and pepper and serve.

SERVES 8 TO 10.

MUSHROOM MORNAY

A cheesy, spicy version of mushroom soup, ideal for weekend lunches in winter.

¹/₄ cup	unsalted butter	50 mL
2 cups	finely diced Spanish onion	500 mL
1 cup	finely diced leek	250 mL
4 cups	sliced mushrooms	1 L
1 tsp	minced garlic	5 mL
¹/₂ tsp	dried sage	2 mL
¹/₄ tsp	dried tarragon	1 mL
1 tbsp	finely diced sweet red pepper or pimento	15 mL
¹/₃ cup	dry white wine	75 mL
6 cups	chicken stock	1.5 L
4 tbsp	beurre-manié	60 mL
¹/₂ lb	grated Swiss cheese	225 g
¹/₄ cup	whipping cream (35 percent)	50 mL
¹/₂ tsp	Worcestershire sauce	2 mL
¹/₄ tsp	ground nutmeg	1 mL
	salt to taste	
	white pepper to taste	

In a large, heavy soup pot, melt butter over medium-high heat until bubbly. Add onion, leek, and mushrooms; sweat until onion is transparent, about 5 or 6 minutes. Add garlic, sage, tarragon, and red pepper and continue cooking 2 to 3 minutes more, stirring occasionally. Stir in wine, bring to boil, and reduce to half the amount. Stir in stock, bring to boil again, reduce heat to medium, and simmer for 5 minutes.

In a medium-sized bowl, whisk beurre-manié until smooth. Slowly whisk in 1 cup (250 mL) of the soup mixture until beurre-manié resembles a smooth paste. Add to the soup 1 spoonful at a time, whisking constantly. Simmer until thickened slightly.

Bring soup back to boil. Add 1 handful of cheese at a time while whisking constantly until melted. Stir in cream and season with Worcestershire sauce, nutmeg, salt, and pepper. Serve immediately.

SERVES 8 TO 10.

FRENCH ONION SOUP

If there exists anywhere a soup more traditionally associated with being indoors on a cold winter evening, complete with blazing logs on the fire, we have yet to hear of it. Hundreds of variations on this standard exist, to be sure, but we think that this is one of the best.

¼ cup	unsalted butter	50 mL
8 cups	sliced Spanish onions (about 4 large)	2 L
2 tsp	minced garlic	10 mL
1 tbsp	tomato paste	15 mL
½ tsp	dried sage	2 mL
½ tsp	dried thyme	2 mL
1 tbsp	brown sugar	15 mL
3	juniper berries	3
½ cup	dry white wine	125 mL
10 cups	chicken stock	2.5 L
1 tbsp	Worcestershire sauce	15 mL
	salt to taste	
	white pepper to taste	
2 cups	grated Swiss or gruyère cheese	500 mL
1 cup	grated parmesan cheese	250 mL
10-12	slices French bread, toasted	10-12
¾ cup	dry sherry	175 mL

In a large, heavy soup pot, heat butter over medium-high heat. Add onions and sauté while stirring constantly until onions turn dark brown, about 10 to 15 minutes. Add garlic, tomato paste, sage, thyme, sugar, and juniper berries, and continue to cook for 4 minutes, stirring constantly. Stir in wine, bring to a boil, and reduce to half the amount. Stir in stock and Worcestershire sauce. Reduce heat to medium and simmer for 30 minutes. Season with salt and pepper.

Preheat oven to 450°F (250°C).

Mix gruyère and parmesan cheeses together in a medium-sized bowl. Bring soup to a boil and fill individual soup terrines ³/₄ full. Top with a slice of French bread and mound ¹/₄ cup of cheese on top of bread.

Bake terrines in preheated oven for 5 minutes or until cheese has melted and turned golden brown color. Remove from oven and spoon 1 tbsp of sherry over the top. Serve immediately.

SERVES 10 TO 12.

This book would not have been possible but for the great support and encouragement from so many people and merchants.

Special thanks to the merchants listed below, as I feel their products are the best in quality and freshness anywhere.

Vinetta Foods	St. Lawrence Purveyors
Phil's Place	Whitehouse and Son
Golden Orchards	Mike's Fish
Uppercut Meats	Rube's
Nick's Meats	NIKI Importing

All are in the historical St. Lawrence Market.

Further thanks to:

Nick Fanais—Corporate manager of the Fish Market Restaurants.

Karen Eastbourne—for her unique penmanship.

Claire Stancer—who helped the beginner along the way.

Family—brother Scott, sister Karan, mother and father.

Nana—just because she is my grandmother.

Mark C.—the fattest man I ever knew.

Peter Taylor—instigator of this project.

Ian Hicks—who was stuck with the mess.

John Delatis—my favourite squash student.

Support and interest from the patrons of Gert's Deli

Special thanks to Chef Domenie Zoffranieri and Chef Herbert Mueller for perseverance, patience and the knowledge they have bestowed upon me.

INDEX